$200

Taiji Sword, Classical Yang Style

Taiji Sword, Classical Yang Style

The Complete Form, Qigong, and Applications

傳統楊氏太極劍

Dr. Yang, Jwing-Ming

YMAA Publication Center
Boston, Mass. USA

YMAA Publication Center
Main Office:
4354 Washington Street
Boston, Massachusetts, 02131
617-323-7215 • ymaa@aol.com • www.ymaa.com

10 9 8 7 6 5 4 3 2

ISBN:1-886969-74-4

Edited by James O'Leary
Cover design by Ilana Rosenberg

Publisher's Cataloging in Publication

(Prepared by Quality Books Inc.)

Yang, Jwing-Ming, 1946-
    Taiji sword, classical Yang style : the complete
    form, qigong, and applications / Yang, Jwing-Ming. --
1st ed.
      p. cm
      Includes index.
      ISBN: 1-886969-74-4

      1. Swordplay. 2. Martial arts. 3. T'ai chi ch'uan
4. Fencing, Oriental.   I. Title.

GV1150.Y36 1999   796.86
                         QBI99-500409

Disclaimer:
The authors and publisher of this material are NOT RESPONSIBLE in any manner
whatsoever for any injury which may occur through reading or following the instructions
in this manual.
The activities, physical or otherwise, described in this material may be too strenuous or
dangerous for some people, and the reader(s) should consult a physician before engaging
in them.

Printed in Canada

Contents

Romanization of Chinese Words. vi

About the Author vii

Foreword by Jeffery A. Bolt xi

Preface xiii

Acknowledgments xv

Chapter 1. General Introduction 一般介紹 1
    1-1. About the Sword
    1-2. Historical Survey
    1-3. Sword Structure
    1-4. The Sword Way
    1-5. About Taiji Sword

Chapter 2. Fundamental Training 基本訓練 20
    2-1. Introduction
    2-2. Hand Grips and the Secret Sword
    2-3. Fundamental Stances
    2-4. Power Training
    2-5. Key Words and Techniques
    2-6. Fundamental Training

Chapter 3. Taiji Sword and Its Applications 太極劍與應用 99
    3-1. Introduction
    3-2. Taiji Sword and Applications

Chapter 4. Taiji Sword Matching Practice 太極劍基本對練 178
    4-1. Introduction
    4-2. Matching Practice

Chapter 5. Conclusion 結論 189

Appendix A. Names of Taiji Sword Techniques 190

Appendix B. Translation and Glossary of Chinese Terms 192

Index 203

Romanization of Chinese Words

This book uses the Pinyin romanization system of Chinese to English. Pinyin is standard in the People's Republic of China, and in several world organizations, including the United Nations. Pinyin, which was introduced in China in the 1950's, replaces the Wade-Giles and Yale systems. In some cases, the more popular spelling of a word may be used for clarity.

Some common conversions:

Pinyin	Also Spelled As	Pronunciation
Qi	Chi	chē
Qigong	Chi Kung	chē kŭng
Qin Na	Chin Na	chĭn nă
Jin	Jing	jĭn
Gongfu	Kung Fu	gŏng foo
Taijiquan	Tai Chi Chuan	tī jě chŭén

For more information, please refer to *The People's Republic of China: Administrative Atlas, The Reform of the Chinese Written Language,* or a contemporary manual of style.

About the Author

Dr. Yang, Jwing-Ming, Ph.D., 楊俊敏博士

Dr. Yang, Jwing-Ming was born on August 11th, 1946, in Xinzhu Xian (新竹縣), Taiwan (台灣), Republic of China (中華民國). He started his Wushu (武術) (Gongfu or Kung Fu, 功夫) training at the age of fifteen under the Shaolin White Crane (Bai He, 少林白鶴) Master Cheng, Gin-Gsao (曾金灶). Master Cheng originally learned Taizuquan (太祖拳) from his grandfather when he was a child. When Master Cheng was fifteen years old, he started learning White Crane from Master Jin, Shao-Feng (金紹峰), and followed him for twenty-three years until Master Jin's death.

In thirteen years of study (1961-1974) under Master Cheng, Dr. Yang became an expert in the White Crane Style of Chinese martial arts, which includes both the use of barehands and of various weapons such as saber, staff, spear, trident, two short rods, and many other weapons. With the same master he also studied White Crane Qigong (氣功), Qin Na (or Chin Na, 擒拿), Tui Na (推拿) and Dian Xue massages (點穴按摩), and herbal treatment.

At the age of sixteen, Dr. Yang began the study of Yang Style Taijiquan (楊氏太極拳) under Master Kao Tao (高濤). After learning from Master Kao, Dr. Yang continued his study and research of Taijiquan with several masters and senior practitioners such as Master Li, Mao-Ching (李茂清) and Mr. Wilson Chen (陳威伸) in Taipei (台北). Master Li learned his Taijiquan from the well-known Master Han, Ching-Tang (韓慶堂), and Mr. Chen learned his Taijiquan from Master Zhang, Xiang-San (張祥三). Dr. Yang has mastered the Taiji barehand sequence, pushing hands, the two-man fighting sequence, Taiji sword, Taiji saber, and Taiji Qigong.

When Dr. Yang was eighteen years old he entered Tamkang College (淡江學院) in Taipei Xian to study Physics. In college he began the study of traditional Shaolin Long Fist (Changquan or Chang Chuan, 少林長拳) with Master Li, Mao-Ching at the Tamkang College Guoshu Club (淡江國術社) (1964-1968), and eventually became an assistant instructor under Master Li. In 1971 he completed his M.S. degree in Physics at the National Taiwan University (台灣大學), and then served in the Chinese Air Force from 1971 to 1972. In the service, Dr. Yang taught Physics at the Junior Academy of the Chinese Air Force (空軍幼校) while also teaching Wushu. After being honorably discharged in 1972, he returned to Tamkang College to teach Physics and resumed study under Master Li, Mao-Ching. From Master Li, Dr. Yang learned Northern Style Wushu, which includes both barehand (especially kicking) techniques and numerous weapons.

In 1974, Dr. Yang came to the United States to study Mechanical Engineering at Purdue University. At the request of a few students, Dr. Yang began to teach Gongfu (Kung Fu), which resulted in the foundation of the Purdue University Chinese Kung Fu Research Club in the spring of 1975. While at Purdue, Dr. Yang also taught college-credited courses in Taijiquan. In May of 1978 he was awarded a Ph.D. in Mechanical Engineering by Purdue.

In 1980, Dr. Yang moved to Houston to work for Texas Instruments. While in Houston he founded Yang's Shaolin Kung Fu Academy, which was eventually taken over by his disciple Mr. Jeffery Bolt after moving to Boston in 1982. Dr. Yang founded Yang's Martial Arts Academy (YMAA) in Boston on October 1, 1982.

In January of 1984 he gave up his engineering career to devote more time to research, writing, and teaching. In March of 1986 he purchased property in the Jamaica Plain area of Boston to be used as the headquarters of the new organization, Yang's Martial Arts Association. The organization has continued to expand, and, as of July 1st 1989, YMAA has become just one division of Yang's Oriental Arts Association, Inc. (YOAA, Inc.).

In summary, Dr. Yang has been involved in Chinese Wushu since 1961. During this time, he has spent thirteen years learning Shaolin White Crane (Bai He), Shaolin Long Fist (Changquan), and Taijiquan. Dr. Yang has more than thirty-one years of instructional experience: seven years in Taiwan, five years at Purdue University, two years in Houston, Texas, and seventeen years in Boston, Massachusetts.

In addition, Dr. Yang has also been invited to offer seminars around the world to share his knowledge of Chinese martial arts and Qigong. The countries he has visited include Canada, Mexico, France, Italy, Poland, England, Ireland, Portugal, Switzerland, Germany, Hungary, Spain, Holland, Belgium, Latvia, South Africa, Morocco, Iran, and Saudi Arabia.

Since 1986, YMAA has become an international organization, which currently includes forty-nine schools located in Poland, Portugal, France, Switzerland, Italy, Holland, Hungary, South Africa, Ireland, Belgium, the United Kingdom, Canada, and the United States. Many of Dr. Yang's books and videotapes have been translated into languages such as French, Italian, Spanish, Polish, Czech, Bulgarian, Russian, Hungarian, and Persian.

Dr. Yang has written twenty-five other volumes on the martial arts and Qigong:

1. *Shaolin Chin Na;* Unique Publications, Inc., 1980.

2. *Shaolin Long Fist Kung Fu;* Unique Publications, Inc., 1981.

3. *Yang Style Tai Chi Chuan;* Unique Publications, Inc., 1981.

4. *Introduction to Ancient Chinese Weapons;* Unique Publications, Inc., 1985.

5. *Qigong for Health and Martial Arts;* YMAA Publication Center, 1985.

6. *Northern Shaolin Sword;* YMAA Publication Center, 1985.

7. *Tai Chi Theory and Martial Power;* YMAA Publication Center, 1986.

8. *Tai Chi Chuan Martial Applications;* YMAA Publication Center, 1986.

9. *Analysis of Shaolin Chin Na;* YMAA Publication Center, 1987.

10. *Eight Simple Qigong Exercises for Health;* YMAA Publication Center, 1988.

11. *The Root of Chinese Qigong—The Secrets of Qigong Training;* YMAA Publication Center, 1989.

12. *Muscle/Tendon Changing and Marrow/Brain Washing Chi Kung—The Secret of Youth;* YMAA Publication Center, 1989.

13. *Hsing Yi Chuan—Theory and Applications;* YMAA Publication Center, 1990.

14. *The Essence of Taiji Qigong—Health and Martial Arts;* YMAA Publication Center, 1990.

15. *Arthritis—The Chinese Way of Healing and Prevention;* YMAA Publication Center, 1991.

16. *Chinese Qigong Massage—General Massage;* YMAA Publication Center, 1992.

17. *How to Defend Yourself;* YMAA Publication Center, 1992.

18. *Baguazhang—Emei Baguazhang;* YMAA Publication Center, 1994.

19. *Comprehensive Applications of Shaolin Chin Na—The Practical Defense of Chinese Seizing Arts;* YMAA Publication Center, 1995.

20. *Taiji Chin Na—The Seizing Art of Taijiquan;* YMAA Publication Center, 1995.

21. *The Essence of Shaolin White Crane;* YMAA Publication Center, 1996.

22. *Back Pain—Chinese Qigong for Healing and Prevention;* YMAA Publication Center, 1997.

23. *Ancient Chinese Weapons;* YMAA Publication Center, 1999.

24. *Taijiquan, Classical Yang Style;* YMAA Publication Center, 1999.

25. *Tai Chi Secrets of the Ancient Masters;* YMAA Publication Center, 1999.

Dr. Yang has also produced the following videotapes:

1. *Yang Style Tai Chi Chuan and Its Applications;* YMAA Publication Center, 1984.

2. *Shaolin Long Fist Kung Fu—Lien Bu Chuan and Its Applications;* YMAA Publication Center, 1985.

3. *Shaolin Long Fist Kung Fu—Gung Li Chuan and Its Applications;* YMAA Publication Center, 1986.

4. *Analysis of Shaolin Chin Na;* YMAA Publication Center, 1987.

5. *Eight Simple Qigong Exercises for Health—The Eight Pieces of Brocade;* YMAA Publication Center, 1987.

6. *The Essence of Taiji Qigong;* YMAA Publication Center, 1990.

7. *Arthritis—The Chinese Way of Healing and Prevention;* YMAA Publication Center, 1991.

8. *Qigong Massage—Self Massage;* YMAA Publication Center, 1992.

9. *Qigong Massage—With a Partner;* YMAA Publication Center, 1992.

10. *Defend Yourself 1—Unarmed Attack;* YMAA Publication Center, 1992.

11. *Defend Yourself 2—Knife Attack;* YMAA Publication Center, 1992.

12. *Comprehensive Applications of Shaolin Chin Na 1;* YMAA Publication Center, 1995.

13. *Comprehensive Applications of Shaolin Chin Na 2;* YMAA Publication Center, 1995.

14. *Shaolin Long Fist Kung Fu—Yi Lu Mai Fu & Er Lu Mai Fu;* YMAA Publication Center, 1995.

15. *Shaolin Long Fist Kung Fu—Shi Zi Tang;* YMAA Publication Center, 1995.

16. *Taiji Chin Na;* YMAA Publication Center, 1995.

17. *Emei Baguazhang, v.1—Basic Training, Qigong, Eight Palms, and Applications;* YMAA Publication Center, 1995.

18. *Emei Baguazhang, v.2—Swimming Body Baguazhang and Its Applications;* YMAA Publication Center, 1995.

19. *Emei Baguazhang, v.3—Bagua Deer Hook Sword and Its Applications;* YMAA Publication Center, 1995.

20. *Xingyiquan—12 Animal Form and Its Applications;* YMAA Publication Center, 1995.

21. *24 and 48 Simplified Taijiquan;* YMAA Publication Center, 1995.

22. *White Crane Hard Qigong;* YMAA Publication Center, 1997.

23. *White Crane Soft Qigong;* YMAA Publication Center, 1997.

24. *Xiao Hu Yan—Intermediate Level Long Fist Sequence;* YMAA Publication Center, 1997.

25. *Back Pain—Chinese Qigong for Healing and Prevention;* YMAA Publication Center, 1997.

26. *The Scientific Foundation of Chinese Qigong;* YMAA Publication Center, 1997.

27. *Taijiquan, Classical Yang Style;* YMAA Publication Center, 1999.

28. *Taiji Sword, Classical Yang Style;* YMAA Publication Center, 1999.

Foreword

I remember my early training with my teacher, Master Yang, the author of this book. Many things he taught me then made more and more sense as my own experience, both as a student and as a teacher myself, increased over time. As in life itself, the martial artist's progression in the beginning is very awkward and rough and the individual is not really sure where this path is leading. For a while, there are always more questions than answers and again, just like life itself, answers are realized with time and experience.

A good teacher will help one to stay on the right path and help the students find out the answers for themselves rather than dictate to him/her the way things should be, which is usually the way that teacher wants it to be rather than the way things are. The teacher can only teach the correct basics; the student himself/herself is totally responsible for the final outcome of all of his/her efforts. The students have freedom to express these basics into whatever form they wish. As long as the proper foundation is present, the expression of what the martial arts mean to a given individual is up to him or her. A good teacher will not restrict the student from this self-expression in the martial arts nor restrict the student in their other life adventures. A good teacher will give this freedom knowing that the real truth lies within the self-expression of the individual and not merely the continued expression of the teacher.

Many teachers will not allow their students to seek knowledge or to learn from others while training in the martial arts. I remember during my first year of training, there were some students who asked Master Yang if they could learn with other teachers at the same time. He told them, "Sure, why not?" Some other classmates who had training from other schools before had told me that their other teachers would never have said that. I have learned, as apparently Master Yang had already known, that the students must choose their own path and make their own decisions. The teacher can teach them what they need to learn regardless of the students' "other" interests.

It is up to the student to figure things out. The students mentioned above eventually dropped their other classes and studied with Master Yang. The students had then made up their own minds and freely chose to stay at our school only—I suspect they might have left our school if Master Yang demanded they study with him only. I have learned that when restrictions are lifted, then the potential of the individual is limitless. I thank my teacher, Master Yang, for teaching me Taiji and giving me the foundation I needed to express myself "my way."

The practicing of Taiji has a great many benefits, one of which is the training of self-expression. This book gives much valuable information about the Taiji sword, which trains the expression of energy from within the body to the sword itself. Many readers will be amazed at all of the detail and specifics that can be learned. Many current practitioners will gain a lot of valuable insight into the uses and applications of their own particular forms even though some of the applications may be different than their own. I'm sure everyone will find this book extremely helpful.

Jeffery A. Bolt
Houston, Texas

Preface

Since the 1960's, Taijiquan has become widely recognized as a valuable exercise and Qigong practice to calm the mind and bring about a healthful, peaceful state. It has also proven to be one of the most effective methods for aiding in the treatment of high blood pressure, depression, hypertension, and cardiovascular problems. In the last few years, it has also been shown to help the elderly regain their balance, both physically and mentally.

Taijiquan was created based on Yin and Yang theory. On the Yang side, it emphasizes maintaining physical strength, especially in the joints and internal organs. On the Yin side, it improves the storage of inner energy (Qi or bioelectricity) through the use of breathing, the concentrated mind and the uplifting of spiritual vitality.

Now, Taijiquan has become a popular practice world-wide. More and more, people are searching for a deeper theory and more pure expressions of this art. Because of this, I have written many Taijiquan books based on my personal study and more than 37 years of experience in Taijiquan practice. The books which I have written are:

1. *Yang Style Tai Chi Chuan*
2. *Tai Chi Theory and Martial Power*
3. *Tai Chi Chuan Martial Applications*
4. *Taiji Chin Na*
5. *The Essence of Taiji Qigong*
6. *Taijiquan, Classical Yang Style*

Now, this new book: *Taiji Sword, Classical Yang Style*. Although barehand Taijiquan and Taiji sword have been introduced in the first referenced book, *Yang Style Tai Chi Chuan* (published by Unique Publications), in the years since its publication in 1982, my understanding and experience have deepened. After 18 more years of practice and teaching, I feel an obligation to clarify and revise certain aspects of my earlier works.

This book contains all new writing and pictures. Revised Taiji sword theory and Qigong practices are also included. Martial applications for each movement are also discussed. However, even though I have tried to make the movements and applications as clear as possible, I still find that the feeling of the art remains missing. This feeling cannot be expressed in words, pictures, or even through video. The profound comprehension of the art comes only from diligent, continuous and regular practice, study, and thought. Learning Taiji is like learning a complex piece of music. The feelings of a musician with 5 years experience can be conveyed so much differently than those of one with 20 years of experience.

The final goal of Taiji practice is to reach this deep level of understanding to live a more enlightened life. If you ignore this ultimate goal, your accomplishments in the art will remain shallow.

In the first chapter of this book, a general introduction will be provided, including a brief history of the sword and the philosophical foundation of sword practice. In the second chapter, basic training for both the external and internal aspects of swordcraft will be discussed. This chapter will help you build up a firm foundation for your Taiji sword practice. Next, the traditional Yang Taiji Sword Form and its applications will be introduced in the third chapter. In order to help you to understand the applications of the sword techniques, several matching sets using the sword will be recommended in the fourth chapter.

Dr. Yang, Jwing-Ming
Boston, Massachusetts

Acknowledgments

Thanks to Tim Comrie for his photography. Thanks to Ramel Rones and James C. Yang for general help with the work. Thanks to Erik Elsemans, Jeffrey Pratt, Ray Ahles, and Sonali Mishra for proofing the manuscript and contributing many valuable suggestions and discussions.

CHAPTER 1

General Introduction
一般介紹

1-1. ABOUT THE SWORD 關於劍

Many martial artists who have studied Chinese martial arts for quite a few years still have a number of questions about the structure, use, history, and geographical background of the Chinese straight sword (Jian, 劍). This is because most students of Chinese martial arts have not also studied Chinese culture. Very little of the available martial literature has been translated into European languages, and the number of qualified and knowledgeable masters is steadily diminishing. This section will discuss general information about the sword. The history and structure of the sword itself, as well as the spirit of Taiji sword, will be discussed in sections 1-2, 1-3, 1-4, and 1-5 respectively.

Definition of the Sword. There are two kinds of weapons commonly called a sword by the Western world. One is the double-edged, straight and narrow-bladed weapon which is called a 'Jian' (劍) in Chinese. The other is the single-edged weapon with a slightly curving, wide blade, which in China is called a 'Dao' (刀). This second weapon will in this book be referred to as a saber. If either of these two types of weapon is shorter than the forearm, it is referred to as a dagger (Bi Shou, 匕首). Daggers can easily be hidden in one's boot or sleeve.

Names of Swords. Chinese swords were often given names. These names usually indicated either the sword's origin or its owner. The origin could be the name of the mountain where the ore used to make the sword, was found (e.g., Kun Wu Jian, 崑峿劍), the place where the sword was forged (e.g., Long Quan Jian, 龍泉劍), or the smith who forged the sword (e.g., Gan Jiang, 干將 and Mo Xie, 莫邪). Of course, the sword could also be named by its owner as he or she pleased (e.g., Judge Dee's sword, 'Rain Dragon' 雨龍). The sword could also be named for the style of sequence for which it was designed to be used (e.g., Taiji Jian, 太極劍).

Names of Sword Sequences. Sword sequences are commonly named for mountains near where the sequence was created, such as Wudang Jian (武當劍); for a division or style of Gongfu (功夫), such as Taiji Jian (太極劍); or for the person who composed the sequence, such as Qi Men Jian (Qi's Family Sword, 戚門劍). They can also be named by the creator of the sequence as he pleases (e.g., Three Power Sword, San Cai Jian, 三才劍).

Functions of the Sword. More than most weapons, the sword serves a variety of purposes. First, the sword has always been used as a defensive, rather than an offensive, battle weapon. Because it is shorter than the spear, the halberd, and many of the other large battle weapons, the sword lacks their long-range killing potential. In battle, the sword was mainly carried for use when the soldier's main weapon was lost or broken. Second, in peace time the sword was treated as a defensive weapon, and was carried by scholars and magistrates, as well as by soldiers. Third, the sword could symbolize the bearer's status. This function of the sword developed to the point that some swords carried by scholars (Wen Jian, 文劍) were so ornate that they could not easily be used for fighting, although this was unusual before the advent of firearms. Fourth, the sword was an integral part of many dances.

Figure 1-1

Why the Sword is Respected. The sword art has been respected in China, not only because the techniques and skills needed to wield it are hard to learn, but more importantly because the morality and spirit of the practitioner have to be of a very high order in order to reach the highest levels of the art. The training is long and arduous, and most people first learn to use other short weapons, such as the saber, in order to build a foundation.

In addition, the sword provides both scholars and martial artists with an elegant feeling and self-respect. It often comes to represent the morality and profound accomplishments in Chinese martial arts that its bearer has achieved. Moreover, since many Chinese emperors in the past specially favored the sword, it has come to symbolize both power and authority in Chinese culture, much as it does in the rest of the world.

Figure 1-2

Carrying the Sword. In China, the sword was either slung from a belt around the waist (Figure 1-1) or hung on the back with shoulder straps (Figure 1-2). The sword could either be carried in a soft scabbard for easy drawing over the shoulder, or a hard scabbard which could be quickly untied from the back for quick access. The way a person carried his sword depended on the weight and length of the sword—double swords and martial swords (Wu Jian, 武劍) were ordinarily carried on the back—as well as personal preference.

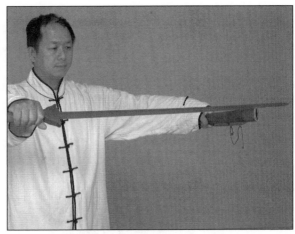

Figure 1-3

How to Inspect a Sword. There are two occasions upon which a sword will be inspected—by the swordsman after using the sword, and by an admirer of the weapon (possibly for purchase). There are several very important conven-

Figure 1-4

tions to be observed when one inspects a sword, and they should be communicated to the neophyte prior to allowing him to handle the weapon. First, the sword is always passed from person to person by handing it hilt first. This minimizes the danger of accidental injury, which is *always* a possibility when dealing with any weapon. Second, the sword handler *never* touches the blade with bare skin, because the sweat-salt and oils from the skin will result in corrosion. Third, the blade is always kept at least eight inches (20-30 cm.) away from the nose and mouth, since moisture from the breath can also result in corrosion of the blade. Fourth, the sword handler never points the sword at another person, both for safety and from courtesy. Fifth, the edge of the blade is inspected by holding the sword by its hilt in one hand and resting the other end against the scabbard (Figure 1-3). If there is no scabbard, the thumbnail of the free hand may be used (Figure 1-4), or even the sleeve (Figure 1-5), so that again, the blade is protected from corrosion. Finally, although it is not a traditional observance, experience has shown that it is not generally a good idea to flourish the sword while inspecting it, as this sort of cavalier treatment of the weapon can often result in accidental injury, especially in crowded areas, and most especially if there are children about. The sword is a dangerous weapon, and it should only be wielded for practice or defense, and *safety* must always be your first priority.

Figure 1-5

How to Select a Taiji Sword. Because of the success of modern metallurgical techniques, there is no longer a need for the student to forge his own sword, as was sometimes necessary in ancient times. Excellent swords can be bought at most martial arts supply stores. A modern sword made from spring steel is the equal or superior of most common swords of antiquity. Plated, untempered swords are also available, and are considerably cheaper than the spring steel variety; however, these are definitely only practice swords. Selection criteria for a Taiji sword are as follows:

Figure 1-6

1. The length, from the tip of the sword to the handle, should be as long as the height from your feet to the base of your sternum (Figure 1-6).

2. The taper of the blade, from hilt to tip, should be smooth and steady, with no abrupt changes in width or thickness.

3. The blade must be straight when viewed down the edge (Figure 1-7).

4. The blade must be firmly mounted in the handle. It should not rattle when you shake it.

5. Spring steel blades must be flexible enough to bend 30 degrees and not retain any bow.

6. The sword should be balanced at a point one third of its length up from the hilt end (Figure 1-8). If it is not, the balance must be altered, or the sword will not handle properly.

7. The tang of the blade (the part of the blade which extends down into the handle) should be as long and as wide as possible. Often, cheaper swords are merely bolted into the handle, and will break easily at this point.

Figure 1-7

8. The quality and finish of the wood and fittings used to construct the sword's handle and scabbard must be adequate. Traditionally, the fittings would be made from brass. Stainless steel might also be a good choice, but I have never seen it used. Cheap wood in the handle and scabbard will quickly crack, rendering the sword useless, no matter how strong its blade.

Sheathing the Sword. Sword and scabbard were formerly created as one interlocking assembly. Many of these units were spring loaded, so that the sword leaped from the sheath when the

Figure 1-8

latch was released. Even when not spring loaded, swords would frequently latch to the scabbard to insure their protection, and these latching scabbards would have a stud at the open end. If you have such a sword, put it away by resting the hilt end of the blade on the stud, drawing the blade out to the tip, and letting the blade slide easily into the sheath. If the scabbard does not have this stud, your thumbnail must serve in its place. The first step in sheathing the sword is to place the thumb over the open end of the sheath so that it is half covered (Figure 1-9), and then bring the sword around, resting the part of the blade closest to the hilt on the thumb and sheath (Figure 1-10). The second step is to slide the sword back along your thumbnail to the tip of the sword, so that the tip will then fall into the end of the sheath (Figure 1-11). Remove the thumb, and slide the sword into the sheath (Figure 1-12). Practice carefully until sheathing the sword becomes natural.

Care of the Sword. In order to protect the sword from damage, the following procedures should be observed:

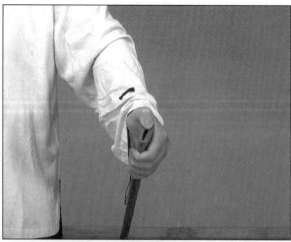

Figure 1-9

1. When you show your sword to someone who knows nothing about it, be sure to tell the person what to do before giving it to him. This will protect your sword, and will also prevent anyone's getting cut.

2. Never lay a sword on the ground. It will absorb moisture from the ground, and in addition somebody might step on it.

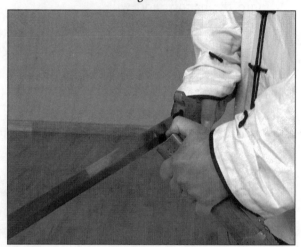

Figure 1-10

3. Never touch the blade with your bare skin. The sweat and oil of your skin will cause the blade to corrode.

4. Avoid unnecessary cutting with the sword, since this will dull the blade and shorten the sword's life.

5. Always keep the sword sheathed when it is not in use.

Figure 1-11

After using the sword, apply a light coating of oil to the blade. Until your level of skill warrants it, don't use a real sword to practice. This will protect you as well as the sword.

Sword Proverbs. There is an old saying that "The staff is the root of all the long weapons, and the saber is the prerequisite for the short weapons,"[1] which implies that the long staff and the saber serve as a foundation for fur-

Figure 1-12

ther work within each group of weapons. In Chinese martial society, it is said that "The spear is the king of the long weapons, whereas the sword is the leader of the short weapons."[2] This saying implies that the spear and the sword are the hardest weapons of their kind to learn, and that once someone can skillfully use them in battle, he/she could quickly understand the techniques and skills needed to wield other weapons, and become the king and leader of any battle. There is another proverb, "A hundred days of barehand, a thousand days of spear, and ten thousand days of sword."[3] From this proverb, one learns that the sword is the hardest weapon of all to learn. This is because the sword is light, and it requires more than ten years of internal power training to master the techniques for blocking heavy weapons. Also, because the sword is double-edged, more skill is required to use both edges effectively without dulling them and/or cutting yourself. Therefore, it is said, "Sword uses speed and technique; saber requires cunning, trickery, and power."[4] It is also said: "Saber, power, won by strength. Sword, soft, won by technique."[5] Finally, it is said, "The saber is like a tiger, the sword is like a phoenix, and the spear is like a swift dragon."[6]

1-2. HISTORICAL SURVEY 劍史

The ancient Chinese regarded the sword as a very important weapon, as evidenced by the relatively large number of documents about it, and the frequency with which swords turn up in archeological digs. It is the only weapon that has been used and admired continuously from the beginning of Chinese history to the present day.

Over time, the sword has evolved from a short, wide copper weapon to a long, slim steel one, resulting from gradual improvements in metallurgy over thousands of years, and the techniques for using the sword have evolved with these changes in structure and quality. The short, wide copper blade would not hold an edge and was soft, so that it could only be used at short range to hack and stab. Bronze is brittle, as is cast iron. Therefore, blades made of these materials would break easily when they were used for blocking. The longer the sword, the longer the effective fighting range, so that the full array of fundamental techniques in use today were only made possible with the discovery of hardened, tempered steel. The number of fundamental techniques increased significantly from a very few with the early short, wide swords, to more than 30 in use today.

In examining the illustrations accompanying this chapter, the reader will notice that swords differed from one dynasty to another, in terms of shape, handle style, and sheath decoration. The changes came about not only because of developments in metallurgy, but also because of the influence of other cultures, particularly those of the invaders of China: the Mongolians (蒙古人), Manchurians (滿州人), Tibetans (西藏人), and Himalayans (喜馬拉亞人). China has in turn been a major influence on the cultures of nearby regions, such as Korea, Japan, and Indo-China. For example, the Japanese Samurai sword may have been originally imported from China during the Tang Dynasty (618-907 A.D., 唐朝), as well as many other weapons which are similar in appearance to those of Tang China.

The Chinese of 3000 to 4000 B.C., like other prehistoric societies, probably used the sticks and stones that lay about them to settle their disputes. Not until the time of the first recorded emperor, Huang Di (2697-2597 B.C., 黃帝), called the "Yellow Emperor" because he ruled the territory near the Yellow River, does evidence exist for weapons made of something other than stone. Huang Di had swords made of jade, copper, and gold. This period, therefore, marks the beginning of the metallurgical science in arms manufacturing in China.

Knowledge of Huang Di's weapons comes from discoveries near Zhuo Lu (涿鹿) of knives and swords, remnants of ancient battles between the emperor's forces and those of Chi Yu (蚩尤).

By the time of the Shang Dynasty (1766-1122 B.C., 商朝) swords made of copper alloys were in use. Bronze ushered in this era, but by its close, iron was being used.

The Zhou Dynasty (909-255 B.C., 周朝) replaced the Shang following fierce warfare. Both emperors demanded better swords, and in this way stimulated advances in metallurgy, although naturally the emphasis was on finding alloys for stronger swords (Figures 1-13 and 1-14). As the power of the Zhou Dynasty diminished over time, the emperor's control weakened, and China was thrust into a series of civil wars. This time is known as the Spring and Autumn Period (Chun Qiu; 722-484 B.C., 春秋) and the Warring States Period (Zhan Guo; 403-222 B.C., 戰國) (Figures 1-15 to 1-18). Each of the many warring factions strove to produce stronger and sharper weapons than before, and swordmakers of the day were held in the highest regard. Three of the most famous swordmakers of that period were Ou Ye Zi (歐冶子), Gan Jiang (干將), and Mo Xie (莫邪).

Ou Ye Zi forged two very famous swords, Ju Que (巨闕) and Zhan Lu (湛盧). It is said that these swords were so sharp that if they were dipped in water, they would be withdrawn perfectly dry. Gan Jiang and Mo Xie were husband and wife, and forged two swords that bore their names.

After Zhou, the Qin Dynasty began (255-206 B.C., 秦朝) (Figures 1-19 and 1-20). When the emperor Qin Shi Huang (221-209 B.C., 秦始皇) took power, he heard that the Wu Emperor (吳) He Liu (闔閭) had collected tens of thousands of swords from all over China, and had them buried with him when he died. Three hundred years later Emperor

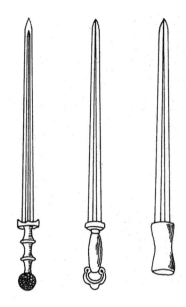

Figure 1-13

Qin Shi Huang ordered his men to find the swords. After many years of searching and digging, the emperor had only a large hole for his efforts. Eventually, the pit filled with water and came to be known as the Sword Pond (劍池) (Figure 1-21) in Suzhou (蘇州).

During the Han Dynasty (206 B.C.-220 A.D., 漢朝) the process of alloying iron instead of copper was first described in the book *Huai Nan Wan Hua Shu* (*Huai Nan's Thousand Crafts,* 淮南萬華術), a book on metallurgy.

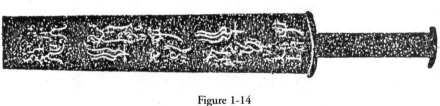

Figure 1-14

Figure 1-15

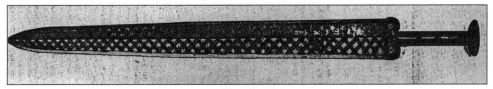

Figure 1-16

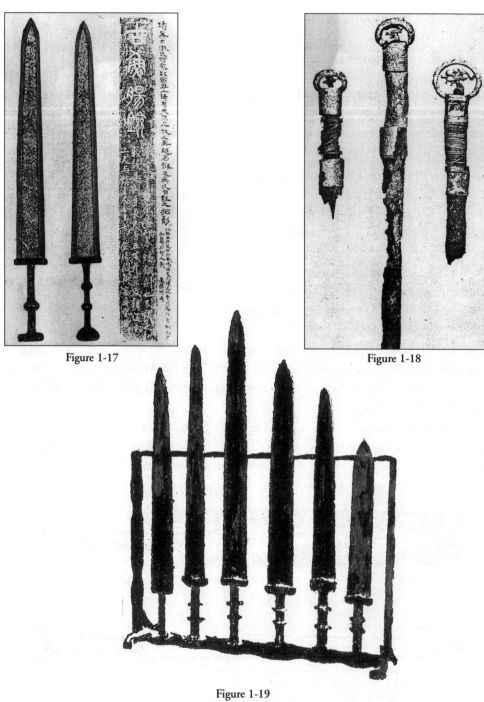

Figure 1-17

Figure 1-18

Figure 1-19

Figure 1-20

The Three Kingdoms Period followed (San Guo; 220-280 A.D., 三國) (Figures 1-22 and 1-23). The famous Cao-Cao (曹操) is reputed to have had swords that could cut iron as if it were mud. There is a story about his rival, Liu Bei (劉備) (Figure 1-24), that illustrates the effect of tempered iron swords. Liu, as a descendant of the Han imperial family, felt he had the duty to reunite China. To do this he occupied Shu (蜀) in western China (Sichuan Province, 四川省), and began preparing his

Figure 1-21

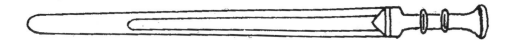

Figure 1-22

Figure 1-23

army for war. To recruit the best fighters, he often held and presided over contests, and one day two fighters stepped forward, one with an iron rod, the other with a saber. During the fight the rod wielder knocked the saber man down and brought his rod down to finish the fight. Everyone present was amazed when the iron rod broke in two as it was blocked by the saber. The maker of that saber, Pu Yuan (浦元) was found and immediately commissioned to forge weapons for Liu Bei.

From the Three Kingdoms Period to the Northern Zhou Dynasty (Bei Zhou; 557-581 A.D., 北周) (Figure 1-25), little is known about the weapons used, although copper is considered to have been the predominant metal in use during this period.

Figure 1-24

The Sui and Tang Dynasties (581-907 A.D., 隋、唐) are the brightest and most peaceful eras in Chinese history. More famous scholars, poets and other artists flourished, while the arts of war were not demanded.

In 907 A.D. the country was once again divided, this time into five parts, known as the Five Dynasties (Wu Dai; 907-960 A.D., 五代). They were later reunited in the Song Dynasty (960-1280 A.D., 宋朝) (Figure 1-26). The Song ended with the invasion of the Mongols (the Jin race, 金) who founded the Yuan Dynasty (1206-1368 A.D., 元朝). This mixing of cultures resulted in more changes in sword styles (Figure 1-27).

In 1368 A.D. the Mongols were defeated by the Chinese, and the Ming Dynasty (1368-1644 A.D., 明朝) began. Then the Manchurians invaded and formed the Qing Dynasty (1644-1911 A.D., 清朝). During these later dynasties, steel and other alloys were used to make swords, which were longer than ever (Figures 1-28 to 1-30). There were three places during the Qing Dynasty which became famous for the quality of their weapons. Two are in Zhejiang Province (浙江省) in eastern China, Long Quan (龍泉) and Wu Kang (武康). The other is Qin Yang (沁陽) in Henan Province (河南省), the site of the Shaolin Temple (少林寺). These places attracted great sword-makers, because of the quality of their water. No one is sure why the water is superior, but great arms have been forged in Long Quan for centuries because of it.

In the eighteenth century, firearms were introduced into China, and further development of the sword as a martial weapon ceased. Consequently, swords and other weapons used for martial arts study remain in the style of the Ming and Qing Dynasties.

1-3. Sword Structure 劍的構造

The sword consists of two parts: the blade and the hilt or handle. Both edges of the narrow blade sword are sharp; the handle and sword body are always straight. The hand guard is always flat, and perpendicular to the blade, rather then being circular or oval.

Figure 1-25

Usually, the sword is one continuous piece of metal, and the hand guard and handle are slipped onto the butt end (the tang) and held in place with a knot-shaped nut or with a pin or rivet. On well made swords, there may also be brass pegs going through the handle and the tang itself. The blade or sword body is sharpened on both edges, and the tip is either rounded or sharply pointed as described below. Swords are from 20 inches to 50 inches long and under 1.5 inches in width.

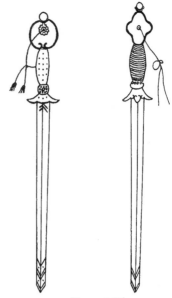

Figure 1-26

The length is divided into three zones. The top third of the blade (Figure 1-31A) is extremely thin and razor sharp. The top third is never used for blocking, because it can be notched very easily. Instead, this sharp part is used only for attack. The middle third of the blade (Figure 1-31B) is thicker and less sharp than the top third. This part of the blade is used for sliding, guiding away, sticking, and cutting. The bottom third (Figure 1-31C) is very thick and unsharpened. The bottom third is usually used for situations when violent blocking is needed. Thus, because of the unique construction of the sword, the Taiji martial artist will attempt to keep his opponent in the middle and long range for proper use of his weapon.

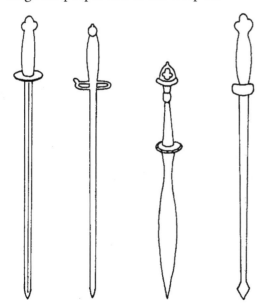

Figure 1-27

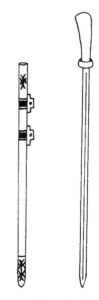

Figure 1-28

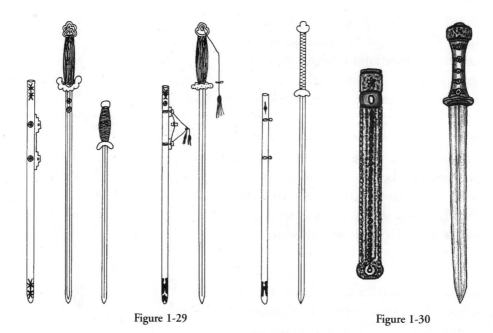

Figure 1-29   Figure 1-30

Types of Swords. Although there are numerous kinds of swords known (Figure 1-32), only five will be described here. Among these, the first two (A and B) are the most common swords, and are the kinds most often used contemporarily for practice. The other three kinds are specialized modifications of the first two. Although they can be used with most common sword techniques, there are additional special techniques made possible by their design.

- A. **Wen Jian** (Scholar's Sword, 文劍): This sword is also called a female sword. It is long and light, with a rounded tip. It is not commonly used for war, but for personal self-defense and for dancing. It was also commonly carried by scholars to present an elegant appearance, or was hung on a wall to decorate a room.

- B. **Wu Jian** (Martial Sword, 武劍): This sword, also known as a male sword, is long and heavy, with a pointed tip (because of its killing potential). It was mainly used in battle.

- C. **Wu Gou Jian** (Wu Hooked Sword, 吳鉤劍): This sword was invented during the Wu Dynasty (222-280 A.D., 吳朝), and is designed for cutting enemies' limbs, or his horses' legs, after blocking a weapon.

- D. **Ju Chi Jian** (Saw Toothed Sword, 鋸齒劍): This sword has a serrated edge to give it greater cutting ability. The edge design probably originated when someone found that a badly nicked blade seemed to cut more viciously. The two holes in the tip of the sword resemble the eyes of a snake, and make a whooshing noise when the sword is swung.

- E. **She She Jian** (Snake Tongue Sword, 蛇舌劍): This sword has a wavy blade, which again makes for a fearful cut. The double point may have given the fighter a way to catch his opponent's weapon at long range.

The Blood Groove (Xue Gou, 血溝). When a sword fighter stabs his enemy, the blade is fixed in the enemy's body by the body's attempt to close the wound. There is also a suction effect on the blade. These factors make it difficult to withdraw the weapon. To solve this problem, most martial swords (Wu Jian, 武劍) were forged with a groove down each side of the blade

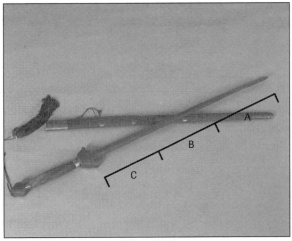

Figure 1-31

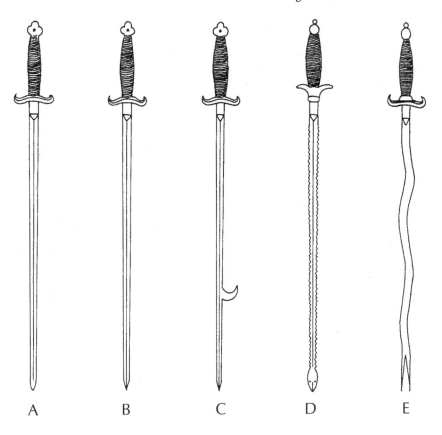

A   B   C   D   E

Figure 1-32

called a blood groove. In battle, one is faced with a multitude of enemies, so the warrior must be able to keep the blade free as much as possible in order to defend himself. Without the blood groove, freeing the embedded sword would require that the swordsman either widen the wound by twisting the blade, or thrust the sword completely through the body to break the suction. The techniques presented later in this book include slashing motions designed to handle this problem.

The Tassel (Jian Sui, 劍繐). Many swords in use today have a tassel hanging from the hilt to enhance their appearance. Generally, this tassel has no martial usefulness for the Jian. However, there are some swords with long tassels (Chang Sui Jian, 長繐劍), where the tassel is designed to attack the opponent's eyes.

Historically, the scholar's sword, the dancing sword, and the decorative sword usually had a tassel, and the martial sword almost never did. The reasons for not using a tassel are as follows: first, the tassel changes the balance of the sword, making it harder to handle; second, it can become entangled in the sword arm and in avoiding this the sword fighter's attention is distracted from the enemy; third, the opponent can grab the tassel and gain control of the sword.

The Sheath (Jian Qiao, 劍鞘). There are two types of scabbard: the scholar sheath and the martial sheath. The scholar sheath is made of wood covered with snake or alligator skin to make it waterproof to protect the sword from moisture. The martial sheath is made of metal to enable it to withstand more abuse, and in addition the metal sheath can be used for blocking. Sheaths should be straight and stiff, and the brackets for the hanger must be tight and not slide up and down the sheath.

Sword Structure and Technique in Relation to Geography. The swords used today are almost all based on Qing Dynasty designs, so only these kinds of swords will be described here.

Northern Chinese tend to be taller than the Southerners, and there are cultural differences as well, which resulted in north/south distinctions in both the structure and techniques of the sword.

Northern characteristics were as follows:

1. Swords are relatively long and narrow (the narrow blade reduces the weight). The average sword is six inches longer than arm length.
2. Sword guards face forward so that the swordsman can lock the opponent's weapon.
3. Northern styles are more offensive or attack-oriented, and specialize in long and middle range fighting.

Southern characteristics, on the other hand, were:

1. Swords are short, averaging arm length, and were relatively wide and thick (to increase the weight).
2. Sword guards slant backward toward the hilt, to slide the opponent's weapon away, in preparation for an attack at close range.

3. Southern fighting styles are more defensive, specializing in short and middle range fighting.

The Taiji sword is generally longer than other northern swords. The regular length of the Taiji sword depends upon the individual. The length should match your height from the feet to the base of the sternum.

1-4. THE SWORD WAY 劍道

In ancient China, the way of the sword was widely respected. This was so not just because sword techniques and skills were difficult to learn. The main reason was that moral and spiritual qualities were required in order to attain the highest levels of its art. In order to build a proper foundation for the study of the sword, the martial artist had to master other short weapons, which meant that he had to spend a long time in preparation. Therefore the sword master (known in China as a Jian Ke, 劍客) had to have willpower, endurance, and perseverance in order to get through the long and hard years of training. It was said that the sword is: "The lord of a hundred arms and the king of short weapons."[7]

Because the sword is mainly a defensive weapon, it requires a strategy of calmness in action, and to achieve this quality one needs patience, calmness, and bravery. Sword users commonly practiced meditation to acquire the calmness they needed. In addition to these qualities needed to develop the required level of skill, sword students learned about ethical virtues from their masters.

The masters would develop these traits in their students by example, and by telling inspiring stories from history. First, a student learned loyalty. The student was taught to be loyal to his country, his master, his parents, and his friends. True loyalty even requires the willingness to die when necessary. Loyalty with honor is the highest form of this virtue. The second trait learned was respect, which is closely related to humility. When one is humble, one can then respect the style, other martial artists, parents, and teacher. Another quality cultivated by the masters, and perhaps the most important, was righteousness. The student was taught to act only in the interests of righteousness and justice.

Having achieved these traits, the sword master is respected by the populace, and will live a life committed to honor.

1-5. ABOUT TAIJI SWORD 關於太極劍

Excepting only Taiji spear, Taiji sword is considered to be the highest level of Taijiquan training. There are a few reasons for this:

1. Before anyone learns Taiji sword, he/she must first master the basic training and criteria for barehand Taijiquan, including correct external forms, relaxed physical body, concentrated mind, proper breathing, and

abundant Qi circulation. Without this foundation, even if a student has learned Taiji sword, his/her level of achievement of this art will remain on the surface. Normally, it will take at least ten years of Taijiquan practice before a person approaches this level of understanding.

2. In order to reach to a deep, profound level of feeling in performing Taiji sword, a student must already have a deep foundation of listening, understanding, sticking, adhering, and coiling Jins. To reach this level of understanding, usually a student must have a few years of correct pushing hands experience. It is well understood that pushing hands is the best way to exchange feeling and sensitivity of the Taiji techniques between you and your training partners. If you practice Taiji sword and try to understand its martial essence, you must learn how to match the sword with a partner. If you are not able to demonstrate the above required Jins from barehand training, you will not understand these Jins as applied in the sword. Again, normally, it will take many years of pushing hands training to reach a deep level of understanding. If you wish to know more about Taiji Jins, please refer to the book: *Tai Chi Theory and Martial Power,* available from YMAA Publication Center.

3. In Taijiquan practice, internal Qigong training is the foundation of internal strength, which can lead you to a deep, profound comprehension of the art. This is especially true in Taiji sword. In order to reach a proficient level of listening, understanding, sticking, adhering, coiling, and neutralizing, your sensitivity and Qi must be able to extend from your physical body to the tip of the sword. You must practice until you feel the sword as a part of your body, natural and comfortable. To reach this level, in addition to performing barehand Taiji Qigong, you should also learn Taiji sword Qigong. We will discuss Taiji sword Qigong in the next chapter.

4. It does not matter if you practice Taijiquan or Taiji sword, the final goal remains the same. You should understand that Taijiquan was created in a Daoist monastery, in which the final goal of spiritual cultivation was enlightenment. In order to reach this stage, you must first ponder, seek out and comprehend the meaning of life. To reach this understanding of life, you must continue to challenge yourself, and master your emotional mind. Self-mastery is a necessary prerequisite for self-understanding. When you have achieved proficient levels of Taiji sword ability, your body will feel transparent (i.e., totally permeable to the energy), and you will be able to enter the state of "mind of no mind" (i.e., regulating without regulating). Every aspect of your practice, from stance to breathing to spirit, is by its nature regulated to the correct level effortlessly, because of the level of skill your practice has brought. Naturally, it is not easy to reach this stage.

When you learn Taiji sword, you first learn the basic sword techniques, which comprise the foundation of each style. In Chinese martial arts, different styles emphasize different techniques, depending on the expertise in which the stylist has trained. For example, the southern sword is relatively shorter in length than the northern sword. Consequently, the sword applications for the southern stylist emphasizes more defense. In comparison, the northern sword is relatively longer, and northern sword users emphasize attacking. External styles have more techniques which are linear and straight forward. Such techniques must be executed externally, requiring more muscular movements. But the basic techniques of internal styles emphasize more sensitivity and Qi cultivation/circulation. Therefore, sticking, adhering, coiling, and circling are the main elements in their practice. In the next chapter, basic sword techniques which are commonly used in Taiji sword will be introduced.

References

1. 棍為長兵之本，刀為短兵之先。
2. 槍為長兵之王，劍為短兵之師。
3. 百日拳，千日槍，萬日劍。
4. 劍走青，刀走黑。
5. 刀、猛、強之以力，劍、柔、勝之以技。
6. 刀如猛虎，劍似飛鳳，槍比游龍。
7. 百刃之君、短兵之王。

CHAPTER 2

Fundamental Training

基本訓練

2-1. INTRODUCTION 介紹

As was mentioned in Chapter 1, the sword is the king of the short weapons. Skilled use of the sword is built on the experience gained from working with the saber, which is called the root of the short weapons. Any martial artist who wants to master the sword should first master the saber, otherwise it will be extremely difficult to understand both the applications of the techniques and the source of power in sword practice.

Although the saber is the root of the short weapons, its techniques and power combinations are very different from those of the sword. For example, the saber uses much muscular power. The dull edge of the saber is designed for blocking vigorously, but this action cannot be done with the sword. Since the sword is double-edged, using either edge to block will dull or nick the blade. With the sword, only that third of the blade nearest the hilt is designed for vigorous blocking. The sharpened part of the blade should not be allowed to contact the opponent's weapon. Therefore, *a defensive attack, without blocking, is the best sword technique, and a sliding block, followed by an attack, is the second best. The least desirable defense is to block using the dull area of the blade.* These concepts will be explained in greater detail in the following chapter.

The fighting strategy is also different between saber and sword. The saber fighter will try to keep the enemy in short and middle range, in order to take advantage of the saber's vigorous blocking and attacking power. To do this, the saber fighter always uses his two hands together. One hand holds the saber, while the other is used for coordination and balance, or to grasp the enemy's wrist, arm, or weapon. The sword fighter, however, tries to keep the enemy in the middle and long range, in order to use the razor sharp tip of the sword effectively. In addition, by keeping some distance from the opponent, it is easier to avoid violent attacks.

For applying power, the saber relies on muscular strength, while the sword uses both the muscles and internal power (Qi) together, in order to defend against a heavy weapon or a strong attack. Because of the more refined nature of the power needed, the sword calls for more technique, more skill, and more training time.

Even though there are so many differences between the saber and the sword, the saber is still the foundation of sword practice. It builds up the stances, dodging, and the basic forward and backward movements. It also builds the muscles required for sword practice. Most importantly, practicing the saber will help the student to understand the general applications and fighting strategies of short weapons.

In learning the sword, the student should first cultivate the virtues of patience and calmness, and develop a firm will. He should understand the form and application of every movement.

In the next section, the ways of holding the sword, and the sword secret hand forms for Qi balance, will be explained. Then, fundamental stances will be covered in section 2-3. Power training for the sword will be in section four. Section five explains the key techniques of the sword. Finally, some fundamental practice forms and drills will be introduced in section 2-6.

2-2. HAND GRIPS AND THE SECRET SWORD 握劍與劍訣

Mastering the sword requires learning to project power into the weapon, but if a person generates power only on one side of the body, disorders will result. To avoid this, sword practitioners hold the empty hand with the index and middle fingers extended, and the thumb folded over the other two fingers (Figure 2-1). When power is extended into the sword, it is also projected from the extended fingers of the empty hand to balance the energy. This is known as the secret sword (Jian Jue, 劍訣). It is also used for applying cavity press when appropriate. There is even an open hand secret sword (Figure 2-2), which is occasionally used in some styles, primarily those in which muscular strength dominates the sword application.

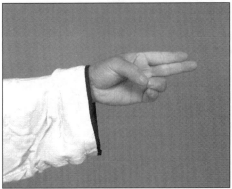

Figure 2-1

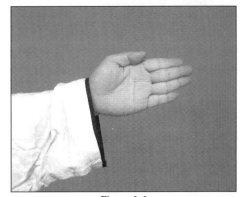

Figure 2-2

There are two basic ways to hold the sword: left-handed and right-handed. The left-handed grip (Figure 2-3 or 2-4) is used at the beginning of sequences, for defensive blocks, and to hold the sword while the right hand is being used for cavity press. The right-handed grip (Figure 2-5) is the usual grip for wielding the sword. Sometimes, when the fingers are too tired to hold the sword single-handedly,

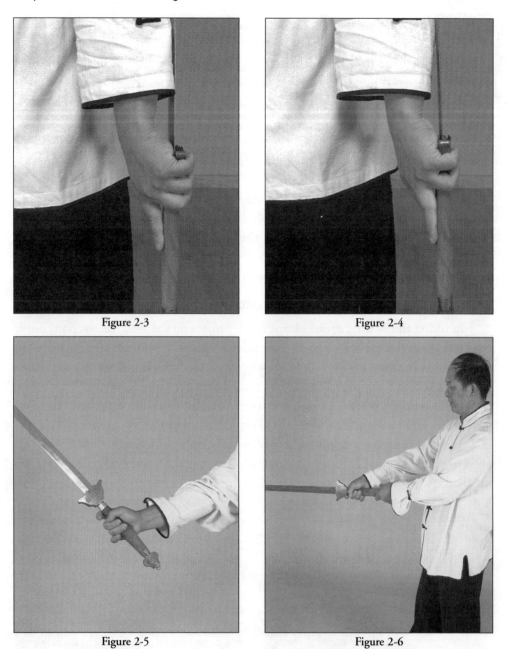

Figure 2-3

Figure 2-4

Figure 2-5

Figure 2-6

a double-handed grip can also be used (Figure 2-6). Correct grip tightness must be maintained. If the grip is too tight, you will lose flexibility and inhibit energy flow. If the grip is too loose, you will not be able to wield the sword swiftly. Either a too tight or a too loose grip make it is easy to be disarmed. The sword should be held like an egg, neither broken nor dropped. The grip should be alive.

2-3. FUNDAMENTAL STANCES 基本庄步

There are six fundamental stances in Taiji sword. The student should become proficient in every one. Each style of Gongfu has its own characteristic stances, and there are variations. Only Taiji stances will be discussed here. It is important to understand that the basic stances are the foundation of the techniques. If the foundation is not firm, then the techniques cannot be performed properly, for they will be unstable. It is the leg forms that are important in the illustrations; the hand forms can vary for the same stance.

1. Horse Stance (Ma Bu, 馬步)

This stance (Figure 2-7) is the most fundamental, and is especially valuable for building up the strength of the knees. To assume this stance, place the feet parallel, slightly beyond shoulder width apart. Bend the knees until a 90 degree angle is formed between the back part of the calf and the thigh, keeping the back straight. It is important to concentrate on directing the power of the legs straight down, like you are standing on stilts, and not to let your weight go out to the sides. The knees should not bow out, and they should be lined up with the toes, which point straight ahead. The beginning student should try to maintain the stance for at least five minutes, but no longer than ten. Only after you have built strong knees should you train to hold the stance for a longer time. You must build up your endurance gradually and slowly.

Figure 2-7

2. Mountain Climbing Stance or Bow and Arrow Stance (Deng Shan Bu or Gong Jian Bu, 蹬山步、弓箭步)

Figure 2-8

This stance (Figure 2-8) is one of the most commonly used offensive stances. About 60 to 70 percent of the weight is on the front leg, and 30 to 40 percent on the rear. The front knee is above the toes, and the back leg is nearly straight. The front shin and calf should be perpendicular to the ground, so that your weight sinks down. It is also important that the toes of your back foot be turned inward slightly, to prevent pressure being put on the ligaments of the inner knee. To prevent knee injury, the knee of the rear leg should be lined up with the toes of the rear foot. The front foot should be turned inward about 15 degrees and the hips should face the direction of the forward leg. The heel of the back leg should remain on the ground, and you should have the feeling of pushing into and through the outer edge of the rear foot (this will help to lift and stabilize the back knee).

Although the rear knee of this stance is described as nearly straight, in most northern external styles, the rear leg for this stance would be held very straight. In Taijiquan practice, the back knee for this stance is kept slightly bent, as is described in the preceding paragraph.

3. Crossed Legs Stance (Zuo Pan Bu, 坐盤步)

This stance (Figure 2-9) can be used either for attack or defense. To assume this stance, first stand in the Horse Stance (Figure 2-10). Raise the right toe while pivoting on the right heel. At the same time, turn right until the body is facing to the rear. During the turn the left foot pivots and turns on its toes (Figure 2-11). Bend the knees until the left knee is about one inch off the ground (Figure 2-12). In this final position, the right foot is flat and the left is on its toes. For turning to the left reverse directions and weighting. Don't rise up during the turn.

4. Four-Six Stance (Si Liu Bu, 四六步)

This is one of the most versatile stances in Chinese martial arts (Figure 2-13). From this stance, the martial artist can switch into various techniques with relative ease. In this stance, 40 percent of the weight is on the front leg, while 60 percent is on the back leg. The knee of the front leg should be turned slightly inward, and be kept slightly bent. Never straighten the knee in this stance, because if a kick were to land on the locked knee, it could easily break it. The front foot should be at a 15 degree angle inward. In addition, the back knee must be flexed and turned inward toward the groin. The back knee and the toes of the back foot should line up with each other. Otherwise, damage to the knee could result.

Figure 2-9

Figure 2-10

Figure 2-11

Figure 2-12

Figure 2-13

Figure 2-14

5. Golden Rooster Stands on One Leg Stance (Jin Ji Du Li, 金雞獨立)

This stance (Figure 2-14) is generally used to set up for quick leg attacks. To assume this stance, raise one leg until the knee is as high as possible. The toes are naturally dropped, relaxed, and comfortable.

6. False Stance (Xu Bu, Xuan Ji Bu, 虛步、玄機步)

This stance (Figure 2-15) can be used for quick kicking. To assume this stance, place all the body's weight on one leg, and lightly touch the ground with the toe of the other. To change legs, turn the body 180 degrees, while shifting the weight from the rear foot to the front foot, which becomes the rear foot. Make sure the lead leg has no weight on it.

Figure 2-15

2-4. POWER TRAINING 功力訓練

General Theory

According to Chinese martial Qigong, the power is first generated from the mind. From the mind, the Qi is led to the physical body to manifest it as power. Therefore, we can see that the Qi is the energy, while the physical body is like the machine. A detailed explanation of Qigong can be found in the YMAA book *The Essence of Shaolin White Crane.*

Furthermore, according to a 1996 article in *The New York Times,* a human being can be thought of as having two brains.[1] One brain is in the head, and the other is in the gut (i.e., digestive system). Though these two brains are separated physically, through the connection of the spinal cord (highly electrically conductive tissue) (i.e., Chinese Thrusting Vessel, 衝脈), they actually function as one (Figure 2-16).

In this article, it is explained that the upper brain is able to think and has memory (i.e., is able to store data, utilizing electrochemical charges), while the lower brain has memory, but does not have the capability of thought. This discovery offers confirmation of the Chinese belief that the Real Dan Tian (i.e., Large and Small Intestines) is able to store Qi (i.e., charges), while the Upper Dan Tian governs thinking and directs the Qi. Theoretically speaking, if the upper brain is able to think, then it should be able to generate an

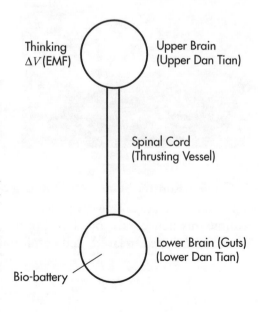

Thinking
ΔV(EMF)

Upper Brain
(Upper Dan Tian)

Spinal Cord
(Thrusting Vessel)

Lower Brain (Guts)
(Lower Dan Tian)

Bio-battery

Figure 2-16

EMF (i.e., electromotive force) while the lower brain should have a large capacity for storing charges. In other words, the lower brain could be the human battery in which the life force resides. Once the brain has generated an idea (i.e., EMF), the charges will immediately be directed from the lower brain, through the spinal cord and nervous system, to the desired area in order to activate the physical body for function.[2]

According to Ohm's Law in Physics,

$$\Delta V = iR$$

where ΔV is potential difference or EMF, i is current, and R is resistance.[3]

From this formula, we can see that if R is a constant, then the higher the potential or EMF, the stronger the current that is generated will be. If we assume that the resistance of our body remains constant, then the more we concentrate (i.e., higher EMF), the stronger the Qi flow will be. This parallels the Chinese Qigong concept that *the more you concentrate, the higher your energy level.* From Chinese Qigong, higher levels of concentration can be trained through still meditation.

We can also examine the formula for physical power manifestation:

$$\text{Power} = \Delta Vi = i^2R$$

This means that the power generated depends on the current and the resistance. Generally, when we intend to manifest our physical strength, for example, when pushing a car, we naturally tense our physical body. Whenever the body is tensed, the resistance of the body is higher, and the energy (current) is trapped in the muscles and power can be manifested. It is the same in many of the external martial styles (or hard styles), such as Tiger and Eagle styles, which focus on building up the muscles (i.e., strong machine) and the tension (i.e., resistance) to manifest power to its highest levels.

However, the concepts and the approaches of the internal styles (or soft styles), such as Taijiquan and Liu He Ba Fa, are quite different. They teach that, since current is the energy of manifestation, and its influence on the power can be much more significant (remember current is squared in the formula), then they should pay more attention to cultivating a stronger flow of Qi. In order to have stronger Qi circulation, meditation is vital, since it generates EMF for moving the current. However, in order to have smooth Qi circulation, physical resistance or tension must be at a minimum. Therefore, physical relaxation is the key to the internal styles.

The best and most focused manifestation of power which can be generated should come from both energy and flesh—the current and the resistance from the above example. Sacrifice either one, and power manifestation is reduced. Therefore, some soft-hard martial styles, such as White Crane and Xingyiquan, emphasize both Qi (current) and tension (i.e., resistance). The way they do so is by first keeping the body as relaxed as possible, while using the concentrated mind to lead the Qi to the physical body, such as the arms or legs. Once the Qi is led from the Lower Dan Tian to the limbs (i.e., right before impact), the physical body will suddenly tense up. Therefore, these styles are called soft-hard styles, and emphasize both internal and external manifestations of power.

From this theoretical perspective, the power generated from the soft-hard styles should be stronger, since it involves both the current and the resistance. However, it is explained in many Chinese martial documents that the power generated in external styles is dull and shallow, but that the power of internal styles is sharp and penetrating. How do internal styles accomplish this? In Chinese internal martial arts, all attacks are targeted at vital acupuncture cavities, which are connected to the internal organs by the Qi channels. When these cavities are struck with fast and focused power, the internal organs can be shocked. The results can be fatal. This is why it is said that internal styles are more penetrating. It is very difficult to accurately strike the vital cavities at the proper depth. This is why internal martial arts are considered to be the highest form of martial arts in Chinese society. It is also the reason that, when a master from an external style has reached a high level, he/she will gradually train to become a soft-hard stylist, and finally will endeavor to become completely soft. In fact, when many masters have reached this stage, they have already become old, and have lost most of their physical strength. In order to survive, changing from hard to soft is almost necessary. If you wish to know more about martial Qigong training, and the different types of martial power, please refer to the books: *The Essence of Shaolin White Crane* and *Tai Chi Theory and Power,* available from YMAA Publication Center.

From the above discussion, you can see that in order to have strong power manifestation, you need to develop both your physical body and your Qi body. Physical strength provides an efficient and strong machine, while an abundant Qi supply provides a pure and powerful energy supply for the machine. Only if you have both can your power be stronger. You will also grow and stay healthy, and your spirit can become uplifted.

In this section, we will first introduce some of the physical practices which can strengthen the muscles and tendons for sword performance. In the next section, training to strengthen the Qi will be discussed.

Physical Training

1. Push-Ups

Figure 2-17

Figure 2-18

Muscular power is developed by strengthening the fingers, the grip, and the arms. The fingers are strengthened by doing push-ups on the finger tips (Figure 2-17). Work up to twenty repetitions. Endurance is developed by holding the push-up position (Figure 2-18) as long as possible, working up to one to three minutes.

2. Bamboo Twisting

Figure 2-19

Figure 2-20

The grip is strengthened by working with bundles of bamboo rods and a training partner (Figures 2-19 to 2-21). Both people turn and raise the bundle in opposite directions. Take turns, one person holding the bundle tightly, the other somewhat loosely, and repeat 50 times. This conditions the palms and helps to strengthen the fingers.

Figure 2-21

3. Windlass

| Figure 2-22 | Figure 2-23 |

This exercise is done using a five to ten pound weight suspended with a cord from the center of a short wooden bar. Stand with the feet well apart and hold the bar straight out at shoulder level. Wind the cord onto the bar, thereby lifting the weight as far as it will go. Slowly lower the weight by unwinding the cord, continue winding the cord to lift the weight again, then lower it to the floor. This set should be performed with the hands held palm down as in Figure 2-22, and with the hands held palm up as in Figure 2-23. Practice winding the weight up and down in both directions at least 10 times. Increase the weight as you are able.

4. Swing Training

Figure 2-24

Figure 2-25

Figure 2-26

Figure 2-27

These three exercises are done using a thick, three foot dowel with a five to ten pound weight suspended from one end. Stand with the feet well apart and hold the stick like a sword. First move the tip from side to side without letting the weight change position, and keeping the handle from moving as well (Figures 2-24 and 2-25). This trains the arm for repelling and covering. Next move the handle end from side to side, while keeping the weight and tip of the stick stationary (Figures 2-26 and 2-27). This trains the arm for sliding and blocking. Finally keep the tip of the stick and the weight stationary and move the hand in a three foot circle both clockwise and counterclockwise. This develops strength and suppleness in the arm. Although these are muscle training exercises, if the student concentrates, he can generate internal energy as well.

5. Accuracy Training

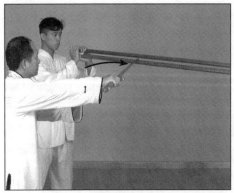

Figure 2-28

Figure 2-29

The student can devise his own methods for learning to cut and thrust accurately. An example of a way to practice cutting is to mount two dowels with a narrow space between them as in Figure 2-28. Practice sliding the tip of the sword between the dowels without touching them. The width of the space between them can be varied, and tape can be used to limit the length of the slit as well, in order to practice cutting to a particular depth, or to practice using the very tip of the sword. Stabbing can be practiced by suspending a small object on a long cord and stabbing it, trying to hit as it swings about (Figure 2-29).

6. Sticking and Coiling Training

Figure 2-30

Figure 2-31

Sticking and coiling with a staff. When you practice the sticking and coiling training, first you should use the staff, since it is easier to feel the contact of your sword and the staff. When you train, simply use the third of the blade nearest the sword tip (see Figure 1-31A) to coil around the staff, without losing contact. You should practice coiling in both directions until you feel comfortable and natural. The motion of coiling must originate from the body, instead of the arms (Figures 2-30 and 2-31).

Figure 2-32   Figure 2-33

Sticking and coiling with a soft branch. This is the same practice as the previous one. The only difference is that you use a soft branch instead of a staff. Therefore, in order for you to coil your sword and adhere to the branch, you must know the level of force you can use. The entire process is to train you to have the feeling of the object through the contact of your sword. You should start with soft power, and go slowly. Make your sword coil around, and whenever the angle is appropriate, use the blade to cut and slide along the branch (Figures 2-32 and 2-33). There should not be resistance between the sword and the branch. Your sword must be like a snake coiling around a tiny branch.

Taiji Sword Qigong

As defined in China, Qi is the universal energy or force existing in this universe. When the concept of Qi is applied to the energy circulating in our bodies, our current best definition of it is bioelectricity. The word Gong is a shortening of the word Gongfu, which is work that consumes time. Therefore, Gongfu can be translated as hard study or discipline. From this, you can see that the meaning of Qigong actually is the study of Qi, or the discipline related to Qi.

In order to use the sword effectively the student must learn to use his/her mind to direct and project the Qi into the sword, balancing the flow of energy with the secret sword hand. This is extremely difficult, and it often takes a life time to reach a high level. In the next section, we will introduce Taiji sword Qigong training. This training was designed for Taiji sword practice. Again, different Taiji styles may have different types of Qigong training. This does not matter; the basic theory remains the same. If you would like to know more about Qigong and Taiji Qigong, please refer to the books: *The Root of Chinese Qigong; The Essence of Taiji Qigong; Taijiquan, Classical Yang Style;* and *The Essence of Shaolin White Crane,* available from YMAA Publication Center.

1. Wuji Breathing (Wuji Hu Xi, 無極呼吸)

This is the process of Dan Tian Breathing. In this breathing technique, first you bring your mind to your Lower Dan Tian so you are able to calm down, and feel your physical and Qi bodies clearly. You should use reverse abdominal breathing—when you inhale, you withdraw your abdomen and gently lift up your perineum (Huiyin cavity), and when you exhale, you expand your abdomen and let your perineum drop. After you practice for about five minutes, your Lower Dan Tian area will be warm, and will feel comfortable. In this process, you are stimulating the Qi at your Lower Dan Tian level to a higher level. It is very important that you keep your mind at this center. Once your mind is away from this center, the Qi will follow, and will flow out of the center and diffuse through the body.

Figure 2-34

When you practice, gently squat down and place both of your palms right on the abdominal area. Center yourself comfortably, and then bring your mind to the abdominal area, while starting to breathe deeply, softly, slowly and smoothly (Figure 2-34). You can remain this way for a few minutes as you feel the Lower Dan Tian area grow warm.

2. Yongquan Breathing (Yongquan Hu Xi, 湧泉呼吸)

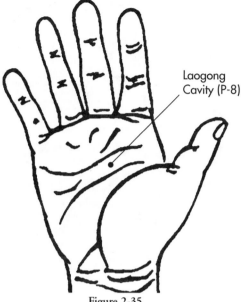

Laogong
Cavity (P-8)

Figure 2-35

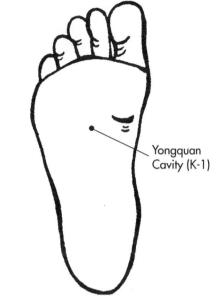

Yongquan
Cavity (K-1)

Figure 2-36

There are four gates on the limbs which are well-known in Chinese medicine and Qigong as cavities (or gates) that regulate the body's Qi state. Two of these gates are Laogong (P-8) (勞宮) located at the center of the palms (Figure 2-35), and the other two are Yongquan (K-1) (湧泉), situated on the front center of the soles (under the feet) (Figure 2-36).

In Chinese martial arts training, learning how to lead the Qi to these four gates and keeping them open is very important. When these gates are open, the Qi will be regulated smoothly and efficiently. This will allow a martial artist to build up his root, and to generate strong power from his hands.

Figure 2-37

In this practice, after you have stored an abundance of Qi in the Lower Dan Tian, when you inhale, you lead the Qi from the Yongquan to the Lower Dan Tian, and when you exhale, you lead the Qi from the Lower Dan Tian to the Yongquan cavities (Figure 2-37). You should practice for several minutes, building up a grounding sensation at the bottoms of your feet.

3. Four Gates Breathing (Si Xin Hu Xi, 四心呼吸)

| Figure 2-38 | Figure 2-39 |

After you have completed a few minutes of Yongquan breathing, you should add breathing to the two Laogong gates at the centers of your palms. When you inhale, use your mind to lead the Qi from the Laogong and Yongquan cavities to the Lower Dan Tian, and when you exhale, lead the Qi to these four cavities at the same time. From the Dan Tian, there are two flows of Qi upward to the palms, and two downward to the bottoms of the feet.

When you practice, place your palms in front of you, with the middle finger slightly forward, to keep the Laogong cavity area relaxed so the Qi can circulate freely. Slightly squat down. In the beginning, keep your mind at the Lower Dan Tian, and inhale deeply (Figure 2-38). Next, squat down slightly deeper when you exhale, and lead the Qi to the four gates (Figure 2-39). In order to lead the Qi to these four gates, you must imagine that you are both pressing your feet and pushing your palms downward. This image will help you to lead the Qi. The more you can concentrate, the stronger the Qi is that you are able to lead. Then, you lead the Qi back to the Lower Dan Tian again when you inhale, to complete the breathing cycle. Perform this breathing for several minutes.

4. Sword Secret Breathing (Jian Jue Hu Xi, 劍訣呼吸)

Figure 2-40

Figure 2-41

After you have become proficient at four gates breathing, you should continue performing it throughout the entire Taiji sword Qigong practice. Eventually, you will want to apply the same breathing technique to the Taiji sword solo form. This breathing technique will lead you to the internal aspect of the art, instead of leaving you with only external forms.

Next, you should not only lead the Qi to the four gates, but you should extend the Qi into the palms, and to the index and middle fingers. Theoretically, the more strongly you are able to lead the Qi out from these two fingers, the more strongly you will be able to lead the Qi to the tip of the sword. When this happens, you will be able to feel the opponent's weapon clearly through your sword. Moreover, you will be able to direct the Qi to the sword tip to execute the techniques.

There are two common practices in this piece. The first is continuing your squat-down position, while placing both of your hands in front of your chest. The palms face in, and the index and middle fingers are gently extended out (Figure 2-40). Again, when you inhale, you lead the Qi from the extremities to the Lower Dan Tian, and when you exhale, you lead it to the feet and the two extended fingers.

After you have practiced for six to ten breathing cycles, when you inhale, keep the same posture, and when you exhale, as you are leading the Qi to the fingers, you also rotate your hands, until the palms are facing forward and downward (Figure 2-41). Again, you should practice for six to ten breathing cycles.

5. Sink the Qi to the Lower Dan Tian (Qi Chen Dan Tian, 氣沉丹田)

Figure 2-42

Figure 2-43

Figure 2-44

The last four pieces are treated as a warm up, encouraging coordination of the mind, body, and breath through concentration, relaxation and smooth, uniform respiration.

Next, inhale and scoop your hands down to the abdominal area, while rotating your hands until they face each other (Figure 2-42). Continue your inhalation, and at the same time raise your hands to chest height (Figure 2-43). The arms are slightly bent. Finally, exhale, rotate both of your hands until they are facing downward, and lower both of your hands to abdominal height (Figure 2-44). You should practice about six to ten repetitions of this up and down cycle.

6. Left and Right Expand the Bow (Zuo You Kai Gong, 左右開弓)

Figure 2-45

Figure 2-46

After you have returned your hands to the abdominal area, next, inhale and raise up both of your hands to the chest area, with both arms lined up (Figure 2-45). Then, continue your inhalation while lowering your elbows (Figure 2-46). Finally, exhale and extend both of your arms to the side horizontally with palms facing forward and fingers extended sideways (Figure 2-47).

Figure 2-47

6. Left and Right Expand the Bow—*continued*

Figure 2-48

Figure 2-49

Next, inhale and bring both of your hands back to the chest area (Figure 2-48) and then exhale and lower both of your arms to your abdominal area (Figure 2-49). Again, you should line up both of your arms when you lower your hands. Perform six to ten repetitions.

7. Left and Right Coil and Turn (Zuo You Chan Zhuan, 左右纏轉)

Figure 2-50   **Figure 2-51**

This piece is very similar to the last one, except that there is a coiling, circular motion in the practice. As with the last piece, first you inhale and lift both of your arms up to the chest area (Figure 2-50). Continue your inhalation while circling both of your hands inward and then to the sides (Figure 2-51).

7. Left and Right Coil and Turn—*continued*

Figure 2-52

Figure 2-53

Finally, exhale and extend both of your arms sideways (Figure 2-52). However, the palms are facing downward this time. Next, inhale and bring your hands back to the chest area (Figure 2-53) and then exhale and bring both of your hands down to the abdominal area (Figure 2-54). Practice six to ten times.

You should always remind yourself that all of the motion in Taijiquan originates from the root (i.e., feet), is directed by the waist (i.e., steering wheel), and finally is manifested in the fingers. Therefore, once you start to move, it does not matter how small a movement you make—it all originates from the body and reaches to the hands. In other words, the hands follow the body's movement, instead of the arms moving independently.

Figure 2-54

8. Arc the Arms for Embracing (Gong Bi Huan Bao, 拱臂環抱)

Figure 2-55

Figure 2-56

Figure 2-57

Figure 2-58

First, inhale and raise up both of your hands to the chest area, with the palms facing upward (Figure 2-55). Next, exhale, lower your hands to the sides of your waist (Figure 2-56), and circle and extend both arms to the sides (Figure 2-57) and then forward to the center of your chest area (Figure 2-58). Both

8. Arc the Arms for Embracing—*continued*

Figure 2-59

Figure 2-60

arms form a circle in front of the chest area. Finally, inhale and bring both hands back to the chest area (Figure 2-59), followed by lowering both hands to the abdominal area while exhaling (Figure 2-60). Practice six to ten times.

9. Fingers on Both Hands Point Forward (Shuang Shou Qian Zhi, 雙手前指)

Figure 2-61

Figure 2-62

Figure 2-63

Figure 2-64

This piece is very similar to the previous one, except that the hands now are extending forward instead of sideways. First, inhale and lift both of your hands to your chest area as before (Figure 2-61). Next, exhale and extend both of your arms forward, with the fingers pointing forward (Figure 2-62). Then, inhale and bring both hands back to the chest area (Figure 2-63). Finally, exhale and lower both hands to the abdominal area (Figure 2-64). Practice six to ten times.

10. Forward and Backward Coil and Turn (Qian Hou Chan Zhuan, 前後纏轉)

Figure 2-65

Figure 2-66

This piece is very similar to the previous piece, except that there is an extra coiling circle right in front of the chest area. Again, inhale and lift both of your hands to your chest area (Figure 2-65). Continue your inhalation while turning your hands inward toward you, and start to turn to point forward (Figure 2-66). Next, exhale and extend both of your arms forward with fingers pointing forward, palms facing downward (Figure 2-67). Then, inhale and bring both of your hands back to your chest area (Figure 2-68). Finally, exhale and lower both hands to the abdominal area (Figure 2-69). Practice six to ten times.

Figure 2-67

Figure 2-68

Figure 2-69

11. Upward and Downward Yin and Yang (Shang Xia Yin Yang, 上下陰陽)

Figure 2-70

Figure 2-71

In this piece, you lead the Qi upward and downward at the same time. First, inhale and bring your left hand up to your face area. Start to turn your hand down, with its fingers pointing downward, while also bringing your right hand upward with its fingers pointing upward (Figure 2-70). Cross both of your hands in front of your chest area and start to exhale (Figure 2-71). Continue exhaling and extend both arms until they are nearly straight (Figure 2-72). Next, inhale and bring your right hand down with its fingers pointing downward, while the right hand raises up with its fingers pointing upward (Figure 2-73). When both hands meet at the chest area, exhale and extend both arms until nearly straight (Figure 2-74). Practice six to ten times.

Figure 2-72

Figure 2-73

Figure 2-74

12. The Fairy Points the Way (Xian Ren Zhi Lu, 仙人指路)

Figure 2-75

Figure 2-76

Figure 2-77

Figure 2-78

Following the previous piece, inhale, lower the left arm across the body until held horizontally across the abdomen, palm facing downward, while raising up the right hand, with fingers pointing upward (Figure 2-75). When the hands meet at the chest area, start to exhale, continue to press the left arm down, and extend the right arm forward (Figure 2-76) until the left hand reaches the abdominal area, and the right arm extends nearly straight out, as you complete the exhalation (Figure 2-77). Next, inhale and move your right hand inward, while lifting your left hand with fingers pointing upward (Figure 2-78). When the hands meet at the chest area, exhale and

Figure 2-79

Figure 2-80

Figure 2-81

Figure 2-82

extend the left arm forward, while lowering the right arm (Figure 2-79). Practice six to ten times.

To finish this practice, inhale and bring your left hand in, and start to lift your right hand (Figure 2-80). When the hands meet at the chest area, allow them to overlap with the palms facing toward you (Figure 2-81). Continue your inhalation, and rotate both of your palms until they face downward (Figure 2-82). Start to exhale

12. The Fairy Points the Way—*continued*

Figure 2-83

Figure 2-84

and lower the arms until they reach the abdominal area (Figures 2-83 and 2-84). Drop both of your hands and relax your fingers. Close your eyes and breathe naturally until you feel comfortable. It is normal if you feel heat on the bottoms of your feet. Simply lift and lower your heels a few times, and the burning feeling will dissipate.

2-5. KEY WORDS AND TECHNIQUES 基本劍法

Generally speaking, due to geographical differences, northern Chinese martial artists have developed techniques which emphasize long and middle range fighting, while southern martial artists focus on firm root, and specialize in short and middle range fighting. Sword techniques which emerged therefore differed according to this developmental influence. For example, the sword techniques of the southern styles emphasize defensive techniques. Therefore, neutralizing, sticking, adhering, and coiling techniques are often the key words or essential secrets of the practice. This is different from those of the northern styles, in which offensive techniques receive more attention. In order to make the techniques most efficacious, the northern sword is relatively longer than the southern sword.

Taiji sword was developed at Wudang mountain (武當山), which is located in Hubei Province (湖北省). This is near the geographic line of division (i.e., Yangtze River, 長江) between the northern and southern styles. It is because of this that

Taiji sword techniques developed there mix both northern and southern elements. Although the length of the Taiji sword used in this region is relatively longer than the ones used in most other styles, the techniques developed still focus on neutralizing, sticking, adhering, and coiling. In one way, the style is extremely offense oriented, but in another, it is very defensive. It is because of this that Taiji sword is well known as one of the most effective sword styles in Chinese martial arts history. It is also because of these unique characteristics that Taiji sword is hard to learn, and even harder to reach its highest levels of understanding and skills.

However, even though there are many different styles which practice sword, the basic theory remains the same. For example, in order to make the techniques effective, internal power must be trained. Moreover, in order to protect the sword from damage (especially the one-third nearest the tip), most of the techniques that were developed are somewhat similar. It is because of this reason that it is fairly easy, once you have mastered one style, to adopt techniques from other styles and blend them into your knowledge and skills.

Before introducing the key techniques for the sword, a few things should be noted. Over all the centuries of its development, many sword techniques were created. Often, due to lack of communication and secrecy, confusion in terminology is common today. Often, the same basic technique has several different names, given by different styles. Occasionally, even techniques with the same name can be slightly or very much different from each other. Therefore, when you start learning these key techniques, you should not be confused and restrict your mind in the areas of terminology and narrow technical meanings. Cast your mind widely, and absorb as much information as possible.

This section will introduce thirty basic sword techniques for your reference and practice. Although many of these techniques are not classified in the Taiji sword basic training, the value of this knowledge is unlimited. It is a wise thing to take advantage of the incredible availability of this knowledge in the world today. Only then can the skill and the knowledge continuously be improved. Often, an open mind is the first key to humble learning. I hope from this introduction, you can begin to grasp the essence of general sword practice.

1. Split or Chop (Pi or Kan, 劈、砍)

Figure 2-85

Figure 2-86

Figure 2-87

Figure 2-88

Pi (split) means to use the top third of the sword blade to split downward, toward the opponent. It is stated in the *Great Dictionary of Chinese Wushu* that: "Pi sword, blade vertical, attack by chopping downward from the top."[4,5] A similar technique can be found as Kan (chop), as stated in the book, *Seven Star Sword* (七星劍): "Kan sword, the sword body is chopping from sideway to forward, to the left, or to the right."[4,6] In fact, vertical downward chopping is also classified as split or chop in many other styles.

Therefore, technically, the motion of this technique can be either vertical (Vertical Chop, Zheng Pi, 正劈) (Figures 2-85 and 2-86) or diagonal (Diagonal Chop, Xie Pi, 斜劈) (Figures 2-87 and 2-88).

2. Stab (Ci, 刺)

Figure 2-89

Figure 2-90

Figure 2-91

Figure 2-92

Ci (stab) means to strike with the tip of the sword in a straight thrust. It is stated in the *Great Dictionary of Chinese Wushu*: "Ci sword, stab forward with vertical blade or horizontal blade. The power reaches the tip of the sword. The arm and the sword line up as a straight line."[4,7]

This technique can be performed with the sword blade vertical, with the palm facing to the left (Vertical Stab, Zheng Li Ci, 正立刺) (Figure 2-89),

Figure 2-93

with the palm facing right (Reverse Vertical Stab, Fan Li Ci, 反立刺) (Figures 2-90 and 2-91), or with the sword held horizontally, either palm up (Horizontal Stab, Zheng Ping Ci, 正平刺) (Figure 2-92) or palm down (Reverse Horizontal Stab, Fan Ping Ci, 反平刺) (Figure 2-93).

2. Stab—*continued*

Figure 2-94

Figure 2-95

Figure 2-96

Figure 2-97

There is another technique which is similar to Ci, called Chong (thrust, 沖). It is stated: "Chong sword, the sword body is moving from the low to the high and straight forward. The sword tip is attacking more forward and less downward."[4,8] Therefore, this technique should be executed as a thrust forward, with the tip of the sword pointing slightly upward (Figure 2-94).

Figure 2-98

3. Slide Upward (Liao, 撩)

Liao (slide upward) means to use the top third of the sword to slide upward and forward to the opponent's body. It is stated in the *Great Dictionary of Chinese Wushu:* "Liao sword, use the sharp place of the sword to slide upward from bottom."[4,9] Naturally, before you can execute this technique, you must first neutralize the incoming attack with other techniques.

This technique can be performed either to the left (Normal Slide Up, Zheng Liao, 正撩) (Figures 2-95 and 2-96) or to the right (Reverse Slide Up, Fan Liao, 反撩) (Figures 2-97 and 2-98).

4. Shake or Sway (Yao, Pao, 搖、拋)

Figure 2-99

Figure 2-100

Figure 2-101

Figure 2-102

It is stated in the *Great Dictionary of Chinese Wushu:* "The sword body moving to the left and right in parallels is called Pao."[4,10] This means to hold the sword blade horizontally, with the palm facing up, and shake the blade from side to side to block or to cut the opponent, while moving either forward or backward. In application, you may neutralize the attack to the left, and then sway to the right to cut the opponent's throat (Figures 2-99 and 2-100). You may also neutralize the attack to your right, and then sway to the left for attack (Figures 2-101 and 2-102).

5. Sweep (Sao, 掃)

Figure 2-103   Figure 2-104

It is said: "Horizontal sword blade, close to the ground, and attacking from left to right or from right to left, is called Sao sword."[4,11] Sao is commonly used to attack an opponent's knees or ankles. The sweeping can be either part of the circle, or the entire circle (Figures 2-103 and 2-104).

6. Intercept (Jie, 截)

Figure 2-105

Figure 2-106

Figure 2-107

Figure 2-108

It is said: "Vertical sword blade, using the tip section of the sword to intercept and attack diagonally upward, downward, or backward, is called Jie sword."[4,12] Technically, Jie is a fast chop to the enemy's wrist, to intercept a stab. If you chop the enemy's wrist internally, it is called an Internal Intercept (Nei Jie, 內截) (Figures 2-105 to 2-107). If you intercept an attack from the outside, it is called an External Intercept (Wai Jie, 外截) (Figures 2-108 and 2-109).

Figure 2-109

7. Pluck (Tiao, 挑)

Figure 2-110

Figure 2-111

Figure 2-112

Figure 2-113

It is stated: "Vertical sword blade, straight arm from the bottom upward, to pluck and attack, is called Tiao sword. The arm and the sword as a straight line (Figures 2-110 and 2-111)."[4,13] Technically, you may use Tiao to attack the opponent's wrist, or to cut upward to the opponent's body (Figures 2-112 and 2-113). For

Figure 2-114

Figure 2-115

Figure 2-116

Figure 2-117

Figure 2-118

Figure 2-119

example, when you block the attack to the inside, and pluck upward to the enemy's wrist from the outside of his arm, it is called an External Pluck (Wai Shang Tiao, 外上挑) (Figures 2-114 to 2-117).

If you block the attack to the side and cut the enemy's wrist from the internal side of his arm, it is called an Internal Pluck (Nei Shang Tiao, 內上挑) (Figures 2-118 and 2-119).

8. Draw Back or Pull (Le, Dai, Chou, Ba, or La, 捋、帶、抽、拔、拉)

Figure 2-120

Figure 2-121

Although there are many different Chinese names for draw back or pull, the basic concepts are the same. It is stated: "Horizontal or vertical sword blade, from the front, pulling (the sword) backward, or upward and backward, is called Dai. The power reaches the sword body."[4,14] It was also explained in the book, *The Great Importances of Wudang Sword Techniques*, that: "Chou, can be distinguished into upper Chou and lower Chou, two kinds. Its action all in situations that the palm holding the sword faces downward, and the back of the palm faces upward. The tip of the sword points forward, and aims at the opponent's upper wrist, or at the lower wrist when pulled toward the right."[4,15]

Technically, this all means to pull the sword backward. You may also use this opportunity to slide on the opponent's wrist while withdrawing. If you draw back from the inside, it is called an Internal Draw Back (Nei Le, 內捋) (Figure 2-120). If you draw back on the outside, it is called an External Draw Back (Wai Le, 外捋) (Figure 2-121).

9. Lift (Gua, 挂)

Figure 2-122

Figure 2-123

Figure 2-124

Figure 2-125

It is stated: "Vertical sword blade, the sword body sliding back for attacking from the front is called Gua sword."[4,16](Figure 2-122) Technically, when your opponent attacks the lower part of your body, you may use Gua to slide the attack backward, to neutralize the attack (Figures 2-123 and 2-124). This motion can also be used to attack after blocking a long weapon, such as a spear (Figure 2-125).

10. Expand (Huo, 豁)

Figure 2-126

Figure 2-127

Huo means to expand. Usually, the sword and the arm are lined up in a straight line. Expand can be done either diagonally or horizontally. For example, when it is used against a stab, first slide block the enemy's sword to the left, then perform the Horizontal Huo to cut the torso (Figures 2-126 and 2-127). Against an attack from the rear, turn around to the right, and use the Huo to cut the enemy's sword wrist, or the back of his neck (Figure 2-128).

Figure 2-128

11. Point (Dian, 點)

Figure 2-129

Figure 2-130

Figure 2-131

Figure 2-132

It is stated for the technique, Dian: "Vertical sword blade, using the lower part of the tip, suspending the wrist and pointing downward for an attack, is called Dian sword."[4,17] Dian is a quick motion that normally aims at the opponent's wrist, neck, or temple. The power of the pointing originates from the jerking of the wrist, and when the tip reaches the target, the wrist is suspended (Figure 2-129).

12. Slide (Fa, 划)

Fa is to use the tip of the sword to slide the opponent. The direction can be up to down, left to right, or front to rear. The key to a successful slide is to keep an effective sliding angle between the sword body and the target (Figure 2-130). For example, after you block the incoming attack, use the tip of your sword to slide to the opponent's throat (Figures 2-131 and 2-132).

13. Smear (Mo, 抹、摸)

Figure 2-133

Figure 2-134

Figure 2-135

Figure 2-136

It is stated: "Horizontal sword blade, using the middle section of the sword body, to pull and slide from the front to the left (or right rear) is called Mo sword."[4,18] It is also stated that: "Mo sword, the sword body horizontal, is the action in which the tip of the sword is pointing forward, and the sword blade is swaying from left to right and from right to left."[4,19] Compared to Slide, the range of attack in Smear is shorter.

Technically, if you deflect the enemy's attack from the inside and then smear the neck, it is called a High Internal Smear (Shang Nei Mo, 上內抹) (Figures 2-133 and 2-134). If you hinder the attack from the outside and then smear the neck, this is called a High External Smear (Shang Wai Mo, 上外抹) (Figures 2-135 and 2-136). If you deflect the enemy's low attack internally and then smear the

Figure 2-137

Figure 2-138

Figure 2-139

Figure 2-140

stomach, it is called a Low Internal Smear (Xie Nei Mo, 下內抹) (Figures 2-137 and 2-138). However, if you slide block the enemy's low attack externally, it is called a Low External Smear (Xia Wai Mo, 下外抹) (Figures 2-139 and 2-140).

14. File (Cuo, 銼、錯)

Figure 2-141

Figure 2-142

Cuo is a technique in which you cut your opponent by thrusting the sword away from you, rather than pulling it toward you. If you file upward, it is called an Upward File (Shang Cuo, 上銼) (Figure 2-141). If you file from the enemy's inside, it is called an Internal File (Nei Cuo, 內銼) (Figure 2-142), and if you file the enemy's wrist from the outside, it is called an External File (Wai Cuo, 外銼) (Figure 2-143).

Figure 2-143

15. Entwine or Wrap (Jiao or Chan, 絞、纏)

Figure 2-144

Figure 2-145

Figure 2-146

Figure 2-147

It is stated: "Circling the sword tip is called Jiao sword."[4,20] (Figure 2-144) Jiao is a technique frequently used to evade a cut to your wrist from your opponent, and cut the enemy's wrist by moving the hand in a circle. If you wrap your enemy's wrist from the outside (counterclockwise), it is called an External Wrap (Wai Jiao, 外絞) (Figure 2-145). If you wrap the enemy's wrist from the inside (clockwise), it is called an Internal Wrap (Nei Jiao, 內絞) (Figure 2-146). This wrist chasing-wrapping-paring technique is also called "Gua Wan" (paring wrist, 刮腕).

Naturally, the circling motion of the sword tip can also be used to wrap the opponent's sword and so neutralize the attack away (Figure 2-147).

16. Bear (Tuo, 托)

Figure 2-148

Figure 2-149

Figure 2-150

Figure 2-151

It is stated: "The sword body strongly blocking upward horizontally, is called Tuo."[4,21] That means Tuo is a strong upward or diagonal block with the thick, dull end of the blade. If you block straight upward, it is called an Upward Bear (Zheng Tuo, 正托 or Shang Tuo, 上托) (Figure 2-148). If you block diagonally, it is called a Diagonal Bear (Xie Tuo, 斜托) (Figure 2-149).

17. Impede or Hamper (Ge, 格)

In the book, *The Great Importances of Wudang Sword Techniques*, it is stated "Ge, is distinguished into lower Ge and flipping Ge, two methods. Lower Ge is the hand holding the sword facing inward, and the sword moving diagonally, from low to high, to cut the opponent's wrist. Flipping Ge is when the opponent is close to the body, dodge his attack, and the hand holding the sword turns the palm from inward to outward, and attacks the opponent's wrist."[4,22]

Therefore, technically, when someone attacks you, squat down to avoid the attack, while using the sword to attack diagonally to his wrist (Figure 2-150). Alternatively, you may dodge to the side and attack the opponent's wrist by turning your hand outward (Figure 2-151).

18. Hinder or Obstruct (Lan, 攔)

Figure 2-152

Figure 2-153

Figure 2-154

Figure 2-155

Lan is the deflection of a stab by sliding the enemy's weapon to the side, away from your body. If you slide block from the inside, it is called an Internal Hinder (Nei Zhong Lan, 內中攔) (Figure 2-152). If you slide block from the outside, it is called an External Hinder (Wai Zhong Lan, 外中攔) (Figure 2-153). If you slide block a low attack internally, it is called a Low Internal Hinder (Nei Xia Lan, 內下攔) (Figure 2-154), and if

Figure 2-156

you block a low attack externally, it is called a Low External Hinder (Wai Xia Lan, 外下攔) (Figure 2-155).

The *Great Dictionary of Chinese Wushu* describes another way to do Lan. It says: "The sword body intercepting (an incoming attack), diagonally from high to low, is called Lan."[4,23] This means that when someone attacks you, you use the middle section of the sword to intercept downward (Figure 2-156).

19. Cloud (Yun, 雲)

Figure 2-157

Figure 2-158

Figure 2-159

Figure 2-160

It is stated: "Horizontal sword blade, circling (the sword) above the head, or upper front of the head, is called Yun sword."[4,24] However, it is stated that Yun can also be done with the blade held vertically. Technically, Yun is mainly a defensive move, used to neutralize an incoming attack with a circular motion of the sword, immediately following the attack (Figures 2-157 to 2-160).

20. Cover and Press Down (Gai and Ya, 蓋、壓)

Figure 2-161   Figure 2-162

In the book, *The Great Importances of Wudang Sword Techniques,* it is stated: "Ya, the palm of the sword-holding hand facing downward, use the sword body to press downward the opponent's sword directly."[4,25] Technically, Ya means to block the opponent's weapon, and immobilize it with a forward and downward push. If you cover from the inside, it is called an Internal Cover (Nei Gai, 內蓋) (Figure 2-161). If you cover from the outside, it is called an External Cover (Wai Gai, 外蓋) (Figure 2-162).

21. Wash (Xi, 洗)

Figure 2-163

Figure 2-164

In the book, *The Great Importances of Wudang Sword Techniques,* it is stated: "Xi, the hand holding the sword turns outward, so the palm faces forward. The sword slides, striking upward with vertical sword blade."[4,26] (Figure 2-163) Technically, Xi can be performed as an offensive attack, right after blocking (Figures 2-164 and 2-165).

Figure 2-165

22. Rise (Jie or Ti, 揭、提)

Figure 2-166

Figure 2-167

Ti means to block the opponent's weapon straight up. Normally, it is followed by straight down chopping (Figure 2-166).

23. Embrace (Bao, 抱)

It is stated that: "Right hand holding the sword, left hand on the side of the handle, is called Bao sword. The sword tip pointing to the right is sideways Bao sword (Figure 2-167); the sword tip pointing upward is vertical Bao sword (Figure 2-168); and the sword tip pointing forward is horizontal Bao sword."[4,27]

Figure 2-168

24. Bore (Chuan, 穿)

Figure 2-169

Figure 2-170

Figure 2-171

Figure 2-172

Chuan means to turn the sword backward, and bore backward to the rear side of the body. When you perform this technique, the power is soft, and the body and the sword coordinate and follow each other (Figures 2-169 and 2-170).

25. Bind (Shu, 束)

It is stated in the book, *The Seven Star Sword,* that: "The sword tip pointing forward, with vertical blade, and the sword body neutralizing backward continuously, is called Shu."[4,28] You may neutralize the incoming attack to your left (Figure 2-171) or to your right (Figure 2-172).

26. Cut (Zhan, 斬)

Figure 2-173

Figure 2-174

Figure 2-175

Figure 2-176

It is stated that: "Horizontal sword blade, attacks sideways to the left (or right), at the height between the head and the shoulder, is called Zhan. The power reaches the sword body and the arms are straight."[4,29] For example, after you intercept the incoming attack, immediately step forward, and use the blade to cut the opponent's throat (Figures 2-173 and 2-174).

27. Block (Jia, 架)

It is stated: "Using the vertical sword blade to block upward, is called Jia sword (Figure 2-175)."[4,30]

28. Sink (Beng, 崩)

It is stated: "Vertical sword blade. Using the sword tip's sharp area to attack (the opponent), from bottom upward along the wrist is called Beng sword (Figure 2-176)."[4,31]

29. Clip (Jian, 剪)

Figure 2-177

Figure 2-178

Figure 2-179

Figure 2-180

It is stated in the book, *The Seven Star Sword,* that: "The sword tip attacking downward, from sideways suddenly, is called Jian."[4,32] You may initiate your attack straight forward (Figures 2-177 and 2-178). Also, after a block, you may hop to the right and at the same time, clip your sword down to attack the opponent (Figures 2-179 and 2-180).

30. Side Cut (Heng, 橫)

Figure 2-181

Figure 2-182

It is stated: "Horizontal sword blade, the action using the sword tip to attack the opponent from sideways (Figures 2-181 and 2-182)."[4,33] For example, you may use this technique to attack the opponent's temple (Figure 2-183).

Figure 2-183

2-6. FUNDAMENTAL TRAINING 基本練習

In order to understand and master the core techniques presented above the student must establish a practice regimen. From the above provided techniques, countless sword skills can be developed. In this section, I will introduce some of the routines that can be constructed from the basic techniques. Most of the following routines are adopted from the Taiji sword sequence that will be introduced in the next chapter. Therefore, if you are able to practice these basic routines first, until they are natural, smooth, and skillful, then you will have accomplished half of the practice requirements needed for Taiji sword practice.

1. Left and Right Horizontal Pull (Zuo You Ping La, 左右平拉)

The main purpose of this training is to teach a student how to control the axial center of the sword. In most of the northern style sword techniques, including Taiji sword, the one-third of the blade nearest the handle is considered to be the axial center. The one-third of the blade which includes the handle is used to generate the coiling and sticking motion, while the other two thirds of the blade are actually used for neutralizing, coiling, sticking, cutting, and stabbing. Remember that the one-third near the handle of the blade is relatively dull, and can be used for violent blocking. The middle one-third is relatively sharper. This section can be used for coiling and neutralizing. The last one-third, near the tip, is razor sharp, and is mainly used for attacking by sliding, cutting, chopping, stabbing, etc. From this, you can see that, in order to coil and neutralize the opponent's weapon, you must be very skillful in handling the sword, and controlling the location of the axial center. When this center is too close to the handle, it is dangerous to you, and if this center is too near the tip, your coiling maneuver will be limited.

Figure 2-184

In this training, you hold your sword with the blade horizontal, then swing from one side to the other while keeping the axial center steady (Figure 2-184). The swinging power is generated from the legs and is directed by the waist. When you swing to one side, inhale, and when you swing to the other side, exhale. The entire body acts as a single unit, and must be as soft as a whip. You should perform at least 50 repetitions before your practice as a warm up exercise. This exercise will help you create a firm foundation for the sticking and adhering of the sword.

2. Left Circle and Twist Sword (Zuo Xuan Jiao Jian, 左旋絞劍)

This basic training is very similar to the previous one, again teaching you how to coil the sword with a circular motion, while keeping the axial center steady (Figure 2-185). When you practice, simply inhale smoothly and naturally. With the same concept, you must generate the motion from your legs, govern it with your waist, and finally manifest it through the sword tip. If you are right handed, this training only focuses on counterclockwise circling. This is because, if you circle clockwise, you will enter the opponent's center area, which is dangerous and undesirable from a practical standpoint. Again, you should practice 50 repetitions as a warming up exercise each time before you train.

Figure 2-185

3. Advance Forward File (Jin Bu Qian Cuo, 進步前銼)

Figure 2-186

Figure 2-187

Figure 2-188

Figure 2-189

In this training, you learn how to slide, or file, the last section of the blade, near the tip, downward and forward. As you are filing, you should step forward (Figures 2-186 to 2-189). When you lift the sword, inhale, and when you file forward and downward, exhale.

4. Left Sweep, Right Sweep (Zuo You Lan Sao, 左右攔掃)

Figure 2-190

Figure 2-191

In this basic training, you first learn how to use the middle section of the sword to block an incoming attack. Then, coordinating the left hand and the stepping, you cut the opponent horizontally at the waist.

When you practice, start with a right horizontal side cut (Figure 2-190). Move your left leg in, next to the right leg, while circling your sword to your left, and move your left hand (in sword secret hand form) to the right wrist. Start to inhale (Figure 2-191). Next, continue your inhaling, circle your sword clockwise in front of you, block your left hand up while stepping to your left, and exhale and slide the sword to your left horizontally (Figure 2-192).

Figure 2-192

4. Left Sweep, Right Sweep—*continued*

Figure 2-193

Figure 2-194

After you have completed the left side, pull your right leg to your left leg, and circle your sword to your right, to block an incoming attack (Figure 2-193). Next, circle your sword in front of you (Figure 2-194), and step your right leg to your right, while sliding your sword to your right, to repeat the training (Figure 2-195).

Figure 2-195

5. Little Chief Star (Xiao Kui Xing, 小魁星)

Figure 2-196

Figure 2-197

This basic training teaches you how to neutralize an incoming attack to the side, and then circle your sword, to slide diagonally upward to the arm pit area. In this practice, the stepping is very important. Only by choosing the correct stepping distance will you be able to perform the technique effectively.

Figure 2-198

In practice, first place your sword diagonally in front of your face, and stand in False Stance (Figure 2-196). Next, move your hand back, and imagine using your sword to block and neutralize an incoming attack to your right, inhale (Figure 2-197). Finally, step your left leg forward, immediately followed by the right leg moving forward into False Stance, while circling your sword back, down, and then diagonally upward to complete the right side, exhale (Figure 2-198).

5. Little Chief Star—*continued*

Figure 2-199

Figure 2-200

Next, lower your handle, while using the sword to block and neutralize an incoming attack to your left (Figure 2-199). Again, the right leg steps first and the left leg follows into False Stance, while your sword circles to your back, down, and then to the right, diagonally upward (Figure 2-200).

6. Right Whirlwind (You Xuan Feng, 右旋風)

Figure 2-201

Figure 2-202

The idea of this training is to chase the opponent's wrist with the razor sharp section of the sword, nearest the tip. In order to make the technique skillful, without risking injury to yourself, the distance between you and your opponent is crucial.

In practice, first circle the tip of the sword at about the circumference of a person's forearm, and imagine that you are cutting an opponent's wrist (Figure 2-201). Now, your opponent must step back to avoid the cut; you immediately step forward while continuing to circle your sword (Figure 2-202). Step the right leg forward to close the range, while again using your sword to cut the opponent's wrist (Figure 2-203). Your breathing strate-

Figure 2-203

gy should be to inhale when you circle the sword around the wrist, and to exhale when you cut the opponent's wrist. Remember, although the circular movement of the handle is big, the circle near the tip of the sword is actually quite small. Again, the entire circular motion originates from your waist.

7. Left Whirlwind (Zuo Xuan Feng, 左旋風)

Figure 2-204

Figure 2-205

This basic training is the reverse of the Right Whirlwind. You step backward this time, and the circle is counter-clockwise instead of clockwise. Again, the entire circular motion is governed by the waist.

In practice, first keep the sword in front of you (Figure 2-204). Next, withdraw your right leg backward, while using the sword tip to cut the opponent's wrist (Figure 2-205). Finally, step your left leg backward as you continue circling your sword, to repeat the exercise (Figure 2-206). Again, when you circle your sword, inhale, and when you cut your opponent's wrist, exhale.

Figure 2-206

8. Part the Grass in Search of the Snake (Bo Cao Xun She, 撥草尋蛇)

Figure 2-207

Figure 2-208

This is one of the main training exercises that teaches you how to stick and adhere with your sword, and then seal your opponent's sword. First, inhale while bringing the sword upright to intercept an attack (Figure 2-207). Next, step your right leg forward, while using the middle section of your sword to stick to the opponent's sword, pressing downward and forward as you exhale (Figure 2-208). Then, bring your sword to your right, to block an incoming attack, and inhale (Figure 2-209).

Figure 2-209

8. Part the Grass in Search of the Snake—*continued*

Figure 2-210

Figure 2-211

Immediately after the block, stick your sword to your opponent's sword, and press downward and forward as you exhale (Figure 2-210). Finally, inhale again, and repeat the first move to continue the exercise (Figure 2-211).

9. The Lion Shakes Its Head (Shi Zi Yao Tou, 獅子搖頭)

Figure 2-212

Figure 2-213

In this basic training, you swing your sword from one side to the other. One side is used to block an incoming attack, and the other side is an attack itself. When you block, inhale, and when you attack, exhale. Again, pay attention to the waist control, and to the distance between you and your opponent.

When you practice, start to step your right leg diagonally to the right, while swinging the sword to your right (Figure 2-212). If you use this swing for a block, inhale. However, if this swing is used to attack, exhale. Next, step your left leg diagonally forward, and then drag the right leg behind you and across the back of your body, while swinging the sword to the left

Figure 2-214

(Figure 2-213). Then, once again step your right leg to the right and forward, and drag the left leg behind and across, while swinging the sword to the right to repeat the exercise (Figure 2-214).

10. Clean Up Dust in the Wind (Ying Feng Dan Chen, 迎風撣塵)

Figure 2-215   Figure 2-216

This exercise is very similar to the training of Open the Grass in Search of the Snake, introduced earlier. The only difference is this time, after intercepting an incoming attack, you stick your sword to the opponent's, and then press directly forward toward his chest area to seal his sword's mobility.

When you practice, first block your sword to your left, with tip facing upward, and move your right leg next to your left leg, as you inhale (Figure 2-215). Immediately after blocking, stick your sword to your opponent's, and press your sword forward to seal his sword right in front of his chest, as you exhale (Figure 2-216).

Figure 2-217

Figure 2-218

Next, turn your body to the right slightly, while blocking your sword to the right, and at the same time step your left leg forward next to your right leg, as you inhale (Figure 2-217). Finally, step your left leg forward while sticking your sword to your opponent's, and press forward toward his chest area to seal his sword's mobility (Figure 2-218).

11. Left and Right Step Over Obstacles (Zuo You Kua Lan, 左右跨攔)

Figure 2-219

Figure 2-220

In this practice, after you block the opponent's attack, use your foot to push the opponent's sword away. This action will only buy you a second, but it allows you to have enough time to circle your sword, and immediately attack your opponent.

To do the technique, first assume a stance with your left leg forward, and your sword as if you have just finished the action of cutting to the left (Figure 2-219). Next, step your right leg beside your left leg while blocking your sword downward, start to inhale (Figure 2-220). Immediately lift your right leg up and circle to your right, continue inhalation (Figure 2-221). Then, step your right leg down while circling your sword, and slide to your right as you exhale (Figure 2-222).

Figure 2-221

Figure 2-222

Figure 2-223

Figure 2-224

Figure 2-225

After you finish the right side cut, pull your left leg in beside your right leg, while blocking your sword to your left as you inhale (Figure 2-223). Next, lift your left leg and circle your leg to your left, start to exhale (Figure 2-224). Finally, step your left leg down while circling your sword, and slide it to the left as you exhale (Figure 2-225).

12. Falling Flowers Posture (Luo Hua Shi, 落花勢)

Figure 2-226

Figure 2-227

This basic training teaches how to neutralize an incoming upper attack, and immediately attack your opponent's arm, or under his armpit. When you block, inhale, and when you attack, exhale. Again, the body's movement, and proper stepping, are very important.

In practice, first assume that you have intercepted an incoming upper attack upward and to the right, while stepping your right leg backward, as you inhale (Figure 2-226). Next, step your left leg backward, while circling the sword back, down, and then sliding up diagonally to the left, as you exhale (Figure 2-227).

Then, use your sword to block an incoming attack to your left, as you inhale (Figure 2-228). Finally, circle your sword back, down, and then slide to the right diagonally, while stepping your right leg backward, as you exhale (Figure 2-229).

Figure 2-228

Figure 2-229

References

1. "Complex and Hidden Brain in the Gut Makes Stomachaches and Butterflies," by Sandra Blakeslee, *The New York Times*, January 23, 1996.

2. *The Second Brain: The Scientific Basis of Gut Instinct and a Groundbreaking New Understanding of Nervous Disorders of the Stomach and Intestine.* Michael D. Gershon, New York: Harper Collins Publications, 1998.

3. *Fundamentals of Physics,* Holliday and Resnick, pp. 512-514. John Wiley & Sons, Inc. 1972.

4. *Great Dictionary of Chinese Wushu* (中國武術大辭典), People's Athletic Publications (人民體育出版社), pp. 287-292, 1990.

5. 〝立劍，由上向下劈擊。〞

6. 《七星劍》：〝劍身由側方，坡向前向左或右為砍。〞

7. 〝立劍或平劍向前直出為刺，力達劍尖，臂與劍成一直線。〞

8. 《中華新武術・劍術科》：〝劍身由下向前向上直行，劍鋒向前多，向下少，為沖。〞

9. 〝用劍的下刃由下向上撩擊稱撩劍。〞

10. 《中華新武術・劍術科》：〝劍身向左或右平行，為拋。〞

11. 〝平劍貼地由左向右或由右向左橫擊掃劍。〞

12. 〝立劍，用劍刃的前端斜面向上、向下、或向後截擊稱截劍。〞

13. 〝立劍，直臂由下向上挑擊稱挑劍。臂與劍成一直線。〞

14. 〝平劍或立劍由前向側後或側後上方抽回為帶，力達劍身。〞

15. 《武當劍法大要》：〝抽，分上抽、下抽兩法。其式均系持劍手手心朝下，手背朝上，劍尖朝前方，對準敵腕之上或下部，往右抽拉。〞

16. 〝立劍，劍身由前向後挂擊稱挂劍。〞

17. 〝立劍，用劍尖下刃，由上向下懸腕點擊稱點劍。〞

18. 〝平劍，用劍身中部由前向左後〔右後〕平腰拉帶稱抹劍。〞

19. 〝摸劍，劍身橫平，劍尖朝前，劍鋒向左右平擺的動作。〞

20. 〝劍尖划圈稱絞劍。〞

21. 《中華新武術·劍術科》：〝劍身由下猛向上橫行，為托。〞

22. 黃元秀《武當劍法大要》釋：〝格，分下格、翻格二法。下格是持劍手手心向內，劍由斜下向斜上格敵腕。翻格是敵近身時閃開其鋒，持劍手由手心向內內旋成手心向外，使劍由下向敵腕翻格。〞

23. 《中華新武術·劍術科》：〝劍身由上向下向左或右斜截，為攔。〞

24. 〝平劍，在頭頂或頭前上方平圓環繞稱雲劍。〞

25. 黃元秀《武當劍法大要》釋：〝壓，持劍手手心向下，使劍身直向下壓敵劍。〞

26. 〝黃元秀《武當劍法大要》釋：洗，持劍手外旋成手心向外，劍面豎直由下向上撩擊。〞

27. 〝右手握劍，左手附于劍柄一側稱抱劍。劍尖朝右為橫抱劍；劍尖朝上為立抱劍；劍尖朝前為平抱劍。〞

28. 《七星劍》：〝劍鋒向前，劍刃向上，劍身連續斜向後帶，為束。〞

29. 〝平劍向左〔右〕橫出，高度在頭與肩之間為斬，力達劍身，臂伸直。〞

30. 〝立劍橫向上格架稱架劍。〞

31. 〝立劍，用劍尖上刃由下向上沿腕崩擊稱崩劍。〞

32. 《七星劍》：〝劍鋒由側突向下擊，為剪。〞

33. 〝平劍，用劍尖橫擊對方的動作。〞

CHAPTER 3

Taiji Sword and Its Applications 太極劍與應用

3-1. INTRODUCTION 介紹

Since Taijiquan has developed for more than a thousand years, various styles have been created. There are many Taiji sword sequences in existence. Nevertheless, all of these sequences have grown out of the same Taiji theoretical roots. Therefore, every movement has its martial meaning and essential feeling. If these are not manifested, the purpose of the movement will not be there, and the meaning of the entire practice will be gone.

Normally, developing this deep feeling of the art will take more than ten years of constant practice. Once this feeling has been comprehended, you can grasp the keys to the techniques. Only then can the art be developed further. There is a well known story about how Zhang, San-Feng taught one of his students Taiji sword:

After a student completed his three years of Taiji sword study with Master Zhang, he was so happy and could perform every movement in exactly the same way as Master Zhang had taught him.

Then, Master Zhang asked him to leave and practice for three years, and then come to see him. The student left. After three years of hard practice, the student came to see Master Zhang. However, he was sad and ashamed to meet Master Zhang. He bowed his head down and felt so sorry. He said to Master Zhang: "Master Zhang, after three years of practice, I am now very sad. The more I have practiced, the more I have lost the feeling I had three years ago. Now, I feel about a third of the forms are different from what you taught me originally."

Master Zhang looked at him and said: "No good! No good! Go home and practice another three years and then come to see me." The student left in sorrow and sadness. He practiced harder and harder for the next three years. Then, he came to see Master Zhang again. However, he felt even worse than the first time he came back. He looked at Master Zhang very disappointedly. He said: "Master Zhang! I don't know why. The more I have practiced, the worse it has become. Now, two thirds of the forms feel different from what you taught me."

Master Zhang again looked at him and said: "No good! No good! Go home again and practice another three years and then come to see me." The student left very very sadly. This time, he practiced even harder than before. He put all his mind into understanding and feeling every movement of the forms he learned. After three years, again he returned to see Master Zhang. This time, his face turned pale and he dared not look at Master Zhang's face directly. He said: "Master Zhang! I am sorry. I am a failure. I have failed you and myself. I feel now not even one form has the same feeling as you taught me."

When Master heard this, he laughed loudly and very happily. He looked at the student and said: "Great! You have done well. Now, the techniques you have learned are yours and not mine anymore."

From this story, you can see that *the mentality of the arts is creative.* If the great composer Beethoven had never learned to create, but had just copied his teacher, then he would not have become so great. It is the same with the great painter Picasso. If he had not known how to be creative, but had allowed himself to be confined by convention, he would never have become such a genius. Therefore, you can see that art is alive, and not dead. However, if you have not learned enough techniques, and have not reached a deep level of understanding, then when you start to create, you will lose the correct path, and the art will be flawed. It is said in Chinese martial arts society: "Sifu leads you into the door, cultivation depends on oneself."

When you learn any art, you should understand *the mentality of learning is to feel and to gain the essence of the art.* Only if your heart can learn the essence of the art will you gain access to its roots. Once connected to this root, you will be able to grow and become creative.

There is another very well known story, about Confucius learning how to play a piece of music for an ancient musical instrument, Gu-Zheng (古箏). Confucius was learning this piece of music from his teacher, Shi Xiang Zu (師襄子). After he finished his learning, he practiced the music for just ten days, yet he was able to perform the music skillfully. His teacher was very happy and asked him: "Are you ready for the second piece?" To Shi Xiang Zi's surprise, Confucius replied: "No!" When Shi Xiang Zi asked him why not, Confucius answered: "Though I am able to play this piece skillfully, I still cannot put my whole feeling into the music, and manifest my feeling through it. Therefore, I prefer to practice for a longer period of time." He practiced this piece of music for several years, until he was able to impart his feelings into the tones of the music. His teacher was very happy about this.

Again, he asked Confucius: "Now, are you ready for the second piece?" Again, the answer was no. His teacher asked: "Why still no, since you are now able to manifest your feelings into the music?" Confucius replied: "Though I am able to play this music with feeling, however, I still don't know the feelings of the composer. When the composer wrote this piece, he put his emotions deeply into it. I must continue my practice until I am able to know the composer's feelings. Again, his teacher left Confucius alone for his own practice.

Three years later, Confucius came to see Shi Xiang Zi and said: "Dear teacher, now I am ready for the new piece." His teacher was very curious and asked: "Does this mean you have learned the feelings of the composer?" Confucius said: "From the music, I can tell he is a six foot tall man. Moreover, he is a person who has such a wide open mind, and such generosity that he is able to ponder the entire heaven and earth." Shi Xiang Zi was so shocked and said: "Amazing, that you can figure this out from the music. You are completely correct. This piece is called "Wen Wang Cao" (文王操) and was composed by King Wen of Zhou (周文王), whose mind was so wide and profound, and he was even six feet tall." According to Chinese history, King Wen of Zhou was six feet tall, and he was the one who interpreted the *Book of Changes* (易經).

From this story, you can see that when you are performing Taijiquan, you are searching for the original motivation of the creator, and trying to achieve the same feeling as the creator. Only then will you touch the root of the forms. We should know that all of the arts are created from the deep spiritual feeling of the creator. When we learn Taijiquan, since we are a beginner in the art, we must follow the knowledge and experiences accumulated by the ancestors. Only after you have mastered all of the forms and techniques passed down to us—like a musician who practices for many years—can you start to blend your own concept and understanding into the art. When this happens, you are creating a new style of art, which derives from an understanding of the past, and is focused through your mind into the present. Therefore, the creative art is alive and developed from deep, profound, internal feeling.

From the above stories, you can see that any pursuit requires a great deal of practice and effort for you to reach a high level of accomplishment. It is this effort that makes it Gongfu (i.e., energy-time, 功夫).

In the next section, I will introduce a traditional Taiji sword sequence. In order to help you grasp the essence of each movement, applications are given. By practicing with the correct feeling of the forms, you will establish a firm root for learning this or any other sword sequence of any internal martial style.

3-2. TAIJI SWORD AND APPLICATIONS 太極劍與應用

Once again, due to the construction of the narrow blade sword and the techniques emphasized by Taiji stylists, there are only a few effective methods for using the sword. Basically, you can slide, sting or stab, deflect cut (sliding and cutting in the same motion), slash, or chop while handling the sword. Most of the motions are done with fluidity and extreme speed. But to properly use each movement of the sword, the stylist must be capable of smooth locomotion. Without the correct use of the legs, each motion of the sword can be wasted. In fact, the ultimate goal of the Taiji swordsman is to successfully attack by never touching the weapon of the opponent through the use of deceptively quick steps.

Like practicing a Taiji barehand sequence, you must learn to coordinate all the forms with deep breathing. The order of the breaths will be in the description of the sequence. The sword forms must be done slowly in order to get the fullness of this elegant and ancient weapon sequence. With patience and practice, the practitioner can make the Taiji sword sequence a useful and beautiful series of techniques for health or defense.

Taiji sword itself is an entire set of advanced Taiji Qigong. After you have learned the entire sequence, sometimes you should practice the entire sequence or even a section of the sequence without holding a sword in your hand. When there is no sword in your hand, physically it is easier to balance. Naturally, it is also easier for your mind to lead the Qi to both arms more evenly and harmoniously. Simply apply the Qigong training concepts with the mind, Qi, and the body's coordination. Soon you will realize that it is as enjoyable as practice with the sword in your hand.

For the purposes of indicating the direction of movement, Chinese martial books use a compass system. The original direction which a person faces is immediately and permanently designated N or North for the duration of the sequence. It does not matter which actual geographic direction the individual faces, the front will always be N. From this designation, the right side becomes E or East, the left side W or West, and back side S or South.

Yang's Taiji Sword Sequence 楊氏太極劍

1. Beginning (Qi Shi, 起勢)

Figure 3-1: (N) The sword is held at the left side and the right palm faces down. The hand form of the right palm is just like that of barehand Taijiquan. The middle finger is slightly forward, while the pinkie and the thumb are slightly backward. Keep your mind calm, and inhale and exhale deeply several times. This is a Wuji state (無極). Keep your mind at your center of gravity (i.e., real Dan Tian, 真丹田).

Figure 3-1

2. Step Forward and Close with Sword (Shang Bu He Jian Shi, 上步合劍勢)

Figure 3-2

Figure 3-3

Figure 3-2: (N) Raise your left knee and turn your right palm to face forward. Begin to inhale.

Figure 3-3: (N) Step forward with your left leg. Raise up your right hand to the side and form it into the Secret Sword Hand. Complete inhalation.

Figure 3-4: (N) Bring your right leg forward into Horse Stance (Ma Bu, 馬步). Move your right hand to your left wrist while bringing your left arm, with the sword, to the front of your body. Exhale.

This is a saluting movement, therefore there are no applications.

Figure 3-4

3. The Fairy Shows the Way-1 (Xian Ren Zhi Lu-1, 仙人指路一)

Figure 3-5

Figure 3-6

Figure 3-5A

Figure 3-6A

Figure 3-5: (W) Turn your body to W while changing to False Stance (Xu Bu, 虚步). Swing the sword across your body, and raise your right hand. Inhale.

Figure 3-5A: As an opponent attempts to stab the abdomen, you slide away the attacker's weapon.

Figure 3-6: (W) Step the left leg forward into Mountain Climbing Stance (Deng Shan Bu, 蹬山步), continue to move your right hand (Secret Sword Hand) to the chest area and then forward with fingers pointing forward. Exhale.

Figure 3-6A: After sliding the opponent's sword away, you attack the opponent's throat with the Secret Sword Hand.

4. **Three Rings Envelop the Moon** (San Huan Tao Yue, 三環套月)

Figure 3-7

Figure 3-8

Figure 3-7A

Figure 3-8A

Figure 3-7: (W) Make a small clockwise circle with your right hand. Begin to inhale.

Figure 3-7A: This technique is used to block a punch or to reverse the situation when the wrist is grabbed.

Figure 3-8: (W) Step forward with your right leg into Crossed Legs Stance (Zuo Pan Bu, 坐盤步). Swing the sword to the front with the handle pointed up. Retreat your right hand to your chest area. Complete inhalation.

Figure 3-8A: From the last blocking, use your sword to push or to cut the opponent's forearm.

Figure 3-9: (N) Continue to bring the sword to the front of your body and then open both of your hands to the sides. The upper body faces N and the face looks E. Exhale.

Figure 3-9A: After blocking in 3-8A, attack the opponent's chin with the handle of the sword.

Figure 3-9B: Your right hand (Secret Sword Hand) can also be used to attack an opponent who attacks you from behind.

Figure 3-9

Figure 3-9A

Figure 3-9B

5. Big Chief Star (Da Kui Xing, 大魁星)

Figure 3-10

Figure 3-11

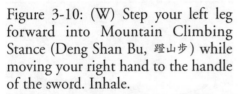

Figure 3-11A

Figure 3-10: (W) Step your left leg forward into Mountain Climbing Stance (Deng Shan Bu, 蹬山步) while moving your right hand to the handle of the sword. Inhale.

Figure 3-11: (NE) Switch the sword to your right hand and then turn NE while sliding the sword to knee level. The left hand stays in touch with your right wrist. Exhale.

Figure 3-11A: You dodge the attack and cut the enemy's knee.

Figure 3-12

Figure 3-13

Figure 3-12: (E) Raise the sword while beginning to draw your left leg up. Inhale.

Figure 3-13: (W) Raise your left knee into The Golden Rooster Stands on One Leg Stance (Jin Ji Du Li, 金雞獨立) while pointing the sword forward and the left Secret Sword Hand to the opponent's third eye. Exhale.

Figure 3-13A

Figure 3-13A: The left hand can be used to block or intercept an incoming attack. The left leg can be used for kicking immediately after the blocking.

6. The Swallow Dips Its Beak in the Water (Yan Zi Chao Shui, 燕子抄水)

Figure 3-14

Figure 3-15

Figure 3-14: (SW) Step your left leg down into Four-Six Stance (Si Liu Bu, 四六步), and at the same time move the sword to the right hand side above the head. Inhale.

Figure 3-15: (SW) Shift the stance forward into Mountain Climbing Stance (Deng Shan Bu, 蹬山步) and slide the sword up. Your left hand touches your right wrist. Exhale.

Figure 3-15A: As the opponent stabs forward, you move to the side and

Figure 3-15A

slide your sword across the neck of the attacker. This is not a hacking motion, but a forward slide. The action shown in Figure 3-14 can be used as a block to deflect the opponent's sword to the side first before your attack to his head.

7. Left Sweep, Right Sweep (Zuo You Lan Sao, 左右攔掃)

Figure 3-16

Figure 3-17

Figure 3-16A

Figure 3-17A

Figure 3-16: (NW) Move your right leg in to the side of your left leg, becoming False Stance (Xu Bu, 虛步) while circling your sword counterclockwise in front of your right hand side. Inhale.

Figure 3-16A: You intercept and slide away an attack to the upper body with the lower third of the sword.

Figure 3-17: (NW) Step your right leg down to the NW while sliding the sword forward and to the right. The stance is Mountain Climbing Stance (Deng Shan Bu, 蹬山步). Exhale.

Figure 3-17A: After blocking in 3-15A, you move in to cut the attacker's waist.

7. Left Sweep, Right Sweep—*continued*

Figure 3-18

Figure 3-19

Figure 3-18A

Figure 3-19A

Figure 3-18: (SW) Bring your left leg in to the side of your right leg and enter False Stance (Xu Bu, 虚步) while moving the sword to the left with tip facing downward. Inhale.

Figure 3-18A: You intercept the opponent's attack by sliding his sword to your left.

Figure 3-19: (SW) Step your left leg down to SW and into Mountain Climbing Stance (Deng Shan Bu, 蹬山步) while blocking your left hand upward and circling your sword clockwise and then slide to your left. Exhale.

Figure 3-19A: After intercepting the opponent's attack, use your left hand to grab or to push away his wrist while circling your sword to your right and then slide your opponent's waist.

8. Little Chief Star (Xiao Kui Xing, 小魁星)

Figure 3-20

Figure 3-21

Figure 3-20A

Figure 3-20: (NW) Raise your sword up to your left while looking to your right. Inhale.

Figure 3-20A: Slide the attack up with the lower third of the sword.

Figure 3-21: (NW) Step forward with your right leg while swinging the sword back. Start to exhale.

113

8. Little Chief Star—*continued*

Figure 3-22: (NW) Continue to swing the sword down, forward, and up while stepping your left leg forward into False Stance (Xu Bu, 虚步). Complete exhalation.

Figure 3-22A: After blocking, step your left leg forward while sliding up into the opponent's arm or armpit area.

Figure 3-22

Figure 3-22A

9. The Yellow Bee Enters the Hole (Huang Feng Ru Dong, 黃蜂入洞)

Figure 3-23

Figure 3-24

Figure 3-23: (NW) Step back with your left leg. Inhale.

Figure 3-24: (SE) Turn your body 180 degrees counterclockwise into Mountain Climbing Stance (Deng Shan Bu, 蹬山步) while stabbing the sword forward and down. Exhale.

Figure 3-24A: As the opponent begins a high attack, you stab low quickly.

Figure 3-24A

10. The Spirit Cat Catches the Mouse (Ling Mao Bu Shu, 靈貓捕鼠)

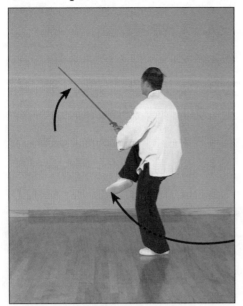

Figure 3-25

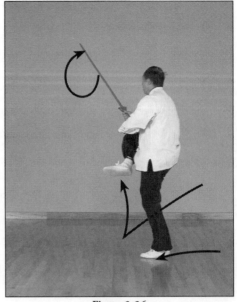

Figure 3-26

Figure 3-25A

Figure 3-25: (SE) Move your right leg up while raising the sword tip up. Begin to inhale.

Figure 3-25A: As the attacker stabs, slide your sword up to block the sword to the right.

Figure 3-26: (SE) Step down with your right leg and jump off it in a forward action. While in the air, move the sword forward, up, and back in a circular motion. Complete inhalation.

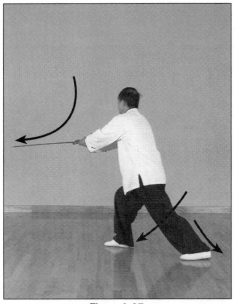

Figure 3-27

Figure 3-27A

Figure 3-27C

Figure 3-27B

Figure 3-27: (SE) Land in Mountain Climbing Stance (Deng Shan Bu, 蹬山步), right leg forward. As the landing is made, stab the sword forward and down. Exhale.

Figure 3-27A: After blocking, immediately stab your opponent. However, if your opponent has a long weapon, you will have to jump forward in order to reach his body (Figures 3-27B and 3-27C).

11. The Dragonfly Touches the Water (Qing Ting Tian Shui, 蜻蜓點水)

Figure 3-28

Figure 3-29

Figure 3-28A

Figure 3-29A

Figure 3-28: (SE) Sit back into Four-Six Stance (Si Liu Bu, 四六步) and raise the sword up in a circular motion. Inhale.

Figure 3-28A: When your opponent attacks your upper body, sit back to avoid the attack while sliding his weapon to your right.

Figure 3-29: (SE) Stab your sword down and forward while shifting your stance to Mountain Climbing Stance (Deng Shan Bu, 蹬山步). Exhale.

Figure 3-29A: Immediately after the block, stab your opponent's waist.

12. The Swallow Enters the Nest (Yan Zi Ru Chao, 燕子入巢)

Figure 3-30

Figure 3-31

Figure 3-30A

Figure 3-31A

Figure 3-30: (N) Slide your right leg back, so that the front of your body is facing directly N, while looking to the E. The stance is False Stance (Xu Bu, 虚步). At the same time that your leg is sliding, turn the sword so your palm faces in and the sword points E. Inhale.

Figure 3-30A: As the opponent attacks, the defender steps back into False Stance (Xu Bu, 虚步) and slides the attacker's sword to the side. The block is made near the lower edge of the sword.

Figure 3-31: (E) Shift the stance into Mountain Climbing Stance (Deng Shan Bu, 蹬山步) while circling the sword up, back, and then forward. Look N. Exhale.

Figure 3-31A: After intercepting your opponent's attack away, step forward and cut his throat.

12. The Swallow Enters the Nest—*continued*

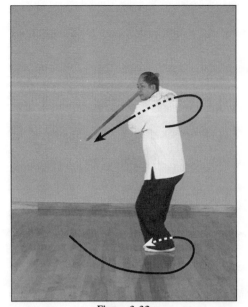

Figure 3-32

Figure 3-33

Figure 3-32A

Figure 3-33A

Figure 3-32: (E) Spin 360 degrees counterclockwise on your left leg while keeping the sword pointing downward diagonally. Inhale.

Figure 3-32A: This technique is used against attacks from a long weapon such as a staff or spear. As the opponent stings with his weapon, you slide the attack away by whirling around. The lower edge of the sword guides the weapon away as the turn is made.

Figure 3-33: (NE) Step your left leg to face NE and slide the sword up. The stance is Mountain Climbing Stance (Deng Shan Bu, 蹬山步). Exhale.

Figure 3-33A: After sliding your opponent's weapon away, you step with your left leg and cut the opponent's neck.

13. The Phoenix Spreads Its Wings (Feng Huang Shuang Zhan Chi, 鳳凰雙展翅)

Figure 3-34

Figure 3-35

Figure 3-34: (SE) Turn 90 degrees clockwise into Horse Stance (Ma Bu, 馬步) while bringing your left hand to the sword. Inhale.

Figure 3-35: (SW) Turn another 90 degrees clockwise into Mountain Climbing Stance (Deng Shan Bu, 蹬山步) while swinging the sword up to your right, palm pointing up. Your left hand retreats to the rear. Exhale.

Figure 3-35A: You dodge an attack and swing the sword up into the opponent's back.

Figure 3-35A

14. Right Whirlwind (You Xuan Feng, 右旋風)

Figure 3-36

Figure 3-37

Figure 3-36A

Figure 3-36: (SW) Step your left leg half a step forward and lift your right heel up into False Stance (Xu Bu, 虛步). While shifting stance, make a small clockwise circle with the handle of the sword, while keeping the tip of the sword fixed in a small circle the size of the wrist. To understand the motion of the sword, the practitioner can press his weapon against a wall and move only the handle in a circle. The wrists must be flexible to make the motion properly. Inhale and exhale.

Figure 3-36A: As the opponent stabs, the defender steps to the side and circles his sword over the attacker's wrist. As the blade circles, the defender cuts into the opponent's wrist.

Figure 3-37: (SW) Bring your legs together and begin the previous sword motion again. Inhale.

Figure 3-38

Figure 3-39

Figure 3-38: (SW) Shift the stance to False Stance (Xu Bu, 虚步) and complete the previously described sword motion. Exhale.

Figures 3-39 and 3-40: (SW) Repeat Figures 3-37 and 3-38.

Figure 3-40

15. Little Chief Star (Xiao Kui Xing, 小魁星)

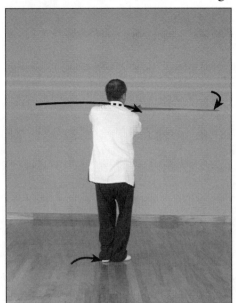

Figure 3-41

Figure 3-42

Figure 3-41: (SW) From the previous form, step your left leg forward while bringing both of your hands together in front of the upper chest. Start to inhale.

Figure 3-42: (SW) Step your right leg forward while circling the sword up and to the left rear. Complete the inhalation.

Figure 3-43: (SW) Step your left leg forward into False Stance (Xu Bu, 虚步) while sliding the sword up diagonally. Exhale.

Figure 3-43

16. Left Whirlwind (Zuo Xuan Feng, 左旋風)

Figure 3-44

Figure 3-45

Figure 3-44A

Figure 3-46

Figure 3-44: (SW) Step your left leg back and drag your right leg in and into False Stance (Xu Bu, 虛步), and circle the handle of the sword in a counterclockwise motion, while keeping the tip of the sword fixed in a circle the size of the wrist. This is the same type of motion as in Right Whirlwind, except that the sword moves counterclockwise. Inhale and exhale.

Figure 3-44A: As the opponent stabs, the defender moves to the outside and cuts down on the attacker's wrist.

Figures 3-45 and 3-46: (SW) Set the right foot down and move backwards with your left leg. As your legs are moving, the sword repeats the counterclockwise circular motion again. Again inhale and exhale.

16. Left Whirlwind—*continued*

Figure 3-47

Figure 3-48

Figures 3-47 to 3-49: (SW) Repeat the circle wrist cutting motion one more time.

Figure 3-49

17. Waiting for a Fish (Deng Yu Shi, 等魚勢)

Figure 3-50

Figure 3-51

Figure 3-50A

Figure 3-51A

Figure 3-50: (W) From the previous backward stepping, bring the sword upward and to the left while drawing your right leg back into False Stance (Xu Bu, 虛步). Your left hand touches the right wrist. The sword is pointing W. Inhale.

Figure 3-50A: The defender slides the opponent's sword to the left.

Figure 3-51: (W) Stab the sword forward and downward. The left hand is extended back. Exhale.

Figure 3-51A: After blocking, the defender stabs the opponent in the belly.

18. Part the Grass in Search of Snake (Bo Cao Xun She, 撥草尋蛇)

Figure 3-52

Figure 3-53

Figure 3-52A

Figure 3-53A

Figure 3-52: (W) Raise the sword up so that the flat part of the blade faces the front of the body. Inhale.

Figure 3-52A: The defender uses the lower part of the sword to guide an attack away.

Figure 3-53: (W) Step your right leg forward so the stance is Mountain Climbing Stance (Deng Shan Bu, 蹬山步). As the weight shifts, slide the sword forward at a level slightly above the knees. Exhale.

Figure 3-53B

Figures 3-53A and 3-53B: The defender steps forward while using his sword to seal and press down the opponent's sword. This will allow the defender to use the left hand to attack.

Figure 3-54

Figure 3-55

Figure 3-54A

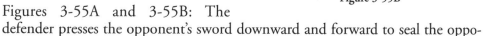

Figure 3-55A

Figure 3-54: (W) Move your left leg to the side of the right leg while blocking your sword to your right. Inhale.

Figure 3-54A: The defender blocks and leads an incoming attack to the right.

Figure 3-55: (W) Step the left leg forward into Mountain Climbing Stance (Deng Shan Bu, 蹬山步) while sealing and pressing down with the sword. Extend your left hand to your left. Exhale.

Figure 3-55B

Figures 3-55A and 3-55B: The defender presses the opponent's sword downward and forward to seal the opponent's sword and immediately uses the left Secret Sword to attack his throat.

18. Part the Grass in Search of Snake—*continued*

Figure 3-56

Figure 3-57

Figures 3-56 and 3-57: (W) Repeat the action shown in Figures 3-52 and 3-53.

19. Hold the Moon against the Chest (Huai Zhong Bao Yue, 懷中抱月)

Figure 3-58

Figure 3-59

Figure 3-58A

Figure 3-59A

Figure 3-58: (W) Draw your right leg back so the stance is False Stance (Xu Bu, 虛步) while turning and raising the sword up and to the left. Inhale.

Figure 3-58A: The defender blocks an incoming attack to the left.

20. Send the Bird to the Woods (Song Niao Shang Lin, 送鳥上林)

Figure 3-59: (W) Step your right leg forward and lift your left knee into Golden Rooster Stands on One Leg Stance (Jin Ji Du Li, 金雞獨立) while spreading the sword and left arm to the sides. Exhale.

Figure 3-59A: Right after blocking in the previous movement, the defender attacks the neck with a sideways motion of the sword.

21. The Black Dragon Waves Its Tail (Wu Long Bai Wei, 烏龍襬尾)

Figure 3-60

Figure 3-61

Figure 3-60A

Figure 3-61A

Figure 3-60: (W) Set your left leg down and draw your right leg back so the stance is False Stance (Xu Bu, 虛步), thigh parallel to the ground. At the same time, bring the sword to the upper chest area. Inhale.

Figure 3-60A: The defender draws in his right leg while using his sword to block an incoming attack.

Figure 3-61: (W) Cut forward and downward with the sword, the right palm faces down and the left hand extends back. Exhale.

Figure 3-61A: After blocking the defender cuts the opponent's leg.

22. The Wind Blows the Lotus Leaf (Feng Juan He Ye, 風捲荷葉)

Figure 3-62

Figure 3-63

Figure 3-62A

Figure 3-63A

Figure 3-62: (W) Turn your body to the right into Crossed Legs Stance (Zuo Pan Bu, 坐盤步) while blocking your sword to your right and up. Inhale.

Figure 3-62A: The defender turns and guides away a high attack.

Figure 3-63: (W) Step with your left leg forward into Mountain Climbing Stance (Deng Shan Bu, 蹬山步) while sliding the sword forward and up. Exhale.

Figure 3-63A: The defender steps in to attack the neck of the opponent after guiding the sword away.

22. The Wind Blows the Lotus Leaf—*continued*

Figure 3-64

Figure 3-65

Figure 3-64A

Figure 3-65A

Figure 3-64: (W) Move the sword inward to the left side. The left hand touches the right wrist. Inhale.

Figure 3-64A: As the opponent attacks, the defender guides the attack away with the bottom edge of his sword.

Figure 3-65: (W) Slide the sword out, palms facing down. Exhale.

Figure 3-65A: After blocking, the defender slashes the neck of the opponent.

23. The Lion Shakes Its Head (Shi Zi Yao Tou, 獅子搖頭)

Figure 3-66: (E) Turn your body 180 degrees clockwise while swinging the sword across the body. Inhale.

Figure 3-66A: When an opponent stabs, the defender pushes the attacker's sword to the side with the lower edge of his sword.

Figure 3-66

Figure 3-66A

23. The Lion Shakes Its Head—*continued*

Figure 3-67: (E) Step your left leg forward and to the side. Move your right leg slightly to the left so that the stance is Mountain Climbing Stance (Deng Shan Bu, 蹬山步). While in the process of moving the body, slash the sword across the front of your body by using the wrists to accomplish this motion. Exhale and then inhale.

Figure 3-67A: After blocking, the defender steps to the side and slashes the opponent's throat with the sword by using a whipping action created by the wrists. This is coordinated with the exhalation.

Figure 3-67B: When the motion in Figure 3-67 is finished, the defender also begins another block, but from an inside position. This is coordinated with the inhalation.

Figure 3-67

Figure 3-67A

Figure 3-67B

Figure 3-68

Figure 3-69

Figure 3-68A

Figure 3-68: (E) Step your right leg forward and to the side. Move your left leg slightly to the right; feet are thus aligned in Mountain Climbing Stance (Deng Shan Bu, 蹬山步). While moving, slash the sword across your body by using only the wrists. Inhale.

Figure 3-70

Figure 3-68A: Once the opponent's sword is neutralized, the defender slashes the attacker's throat.

Figures 3-69 and 3-70: (E) Repeat Figures 3-67 and 3-68. Exhale and Inhale.

24. The Tiger Holds Its Head (Hu Bao Tou, 虎抱頭)

Figure 3-71

Figure 3-72

Figure 3-71: Slide your sword from the right to the front. Exhale.

Figure 3-72: (E) Draw the sword in and shift the stance to False Stance (Xu Bu, 虚步). Inhale.

Figure 3-72A: The defender withdraws his sword left while using it to block an incoming attack.

Figure 3-72A

25. The Wild Horse Jumps the Stream (Ye Ma Tiao Jian, 野馬跳澗)

Figure 3-73

Figure 3-74

Figure 3-73: (E) Step down with the right leg and immediately jump off the ground while circling your sword. Start to exhale.

Figure 3-74: (E) Land into Mountain Climbing Stance (Deng Shan Bu, 蹬山步) while stabbing the sword forward and downward. Complete exhalation.

Figure 3-74A: After blocking from the previous posture, the defender jumps into closer range and stabs the opponent with the sword.

Figure 3-74A

26. Turn Body and Rein In the Horse (Fan Shen Le Ma, 翻身勒馬)

Figure 3-75

Figure 3-76

Figure 3-75A

Figure 3-76A

Figure 3-75: (W) Turn your body 180 degrees counterclockwise into Mountain Climbing Stance (Deng Shan Bu, 蹬山步) while swinging your left hand across your body. Inhale.

Figure 3-75A: As an opponent attacks with a long weapon, the defender pushes it to the side and grabs it.

Figure 3-76: (W) Swing the sword all the way around to the left hand. Exhale.

Figure 3-76A: Following the interception, the defender cuts the attacker's neck.

Figure 3-77   Figure 3-78

Figure 3-77A   Figure 3-78A

Figure 3-77: (W) Draw in the sword and left leg and shift into False Stance (Xu Bu, 虛步). Inhale.

Figure 3-77A: When the defender is attacked, he slides his sword over the opponent's wrist.

27. Compass (Zhi Nan Zhen, 指南針)

Figure 3-78: (W) Bring your right leg up and stab the sword forward while squatting. Exhale.

Figure 3-78A: Once the wrist has been cut, the defender moves in to stab the throat.

28. Clean Up Dust in the Wind (Ying Feng Dan Chen, 迎風撣塵)

Figure 3-79

Figure 3-80

Figure 3-79A

Figure 3-80A

Figure 3-79: (W) Turn your body to your left slightly while lifting your sword to your left. Right palm faces inward. Inhale.

Figure 3-79A: The defender blocks an attack with the lower edge of his sword.

Figure 3-80: (W) Step your right leg forward into Mountain Climbing Stance (Deng Shan Bu, 蹬山步) while pushing the sword forward from your chest. Exhale.

Figure 3-80A: Once the block is complete, the defender slides in and strikes the opponent's fingers with the lower edge of the sword. The defender thus hits, rather than cuts, the opponent. This technique is also commonly used to seal the opponent's weapon.

Figure 3-81

Figure 3-82

Figure 3-81A

Figure 3-82A

Figure 3-81: (W) Step your left leg to the side of your right leg and turn the sword up and to the right. The right palm faces the right. Inhale.

Figure 3-81A: The defender blocks an attack to the right.

Figure 3-82: (W) Step your left leg out and push the sword forward from your chest. The stance is Mountain Climbing Stance (Deng Shan Bu, 蹬山步). Exhale.

Figure 3-82A: After the block, the defender slides and pushes the sword forward to cut the opponent's finger. Again, this technique can be used to seal the opponent's weapon.

28. Clean Up Dust in the Wind—*continued*

Figure 3-83

Figure 3-84

Figures 3-83 and 3-84: Repeat Figures 3-79 and 3-80.

29. Push the Boat with the Current (Shun Shui Tui Zhou, 順水推舟)

Figure 3-85

Figure 3-86

Figure 3-85A

Figure 3-85: (W) Move your right leg to the left side half of a step so that it crosses your left leg. At the same time, slide the sword down to where the right leg was originally positioned. Start to inhale.

Figure 3-85A: The defender slides away an attack to his lower body.

Figure 3-86: Step your left leg forward into Mountain Climbing Stance (Deng Shan Bu, 蹬山步), open your left arm, while swinging the sword back and up. Complete inhalation.

29. Push the Boat with the Current—*continued*

Figure 3-87

Figure 3-88

Figure 3-87A

Figure 3-88A

Figure 3-87: (W) Move the tip of the sword forward while moving your left hand to the right wrist area. Exhale.

Figure 3-87A: Once the low attack is guided away, the defender steps in to stab the opponent from the top. The left hand is used to seal the opponent's right arm.

30. The Shooting Star Chasing the Moon (Liu Xing Gan Yue, 流星趕月)

Figure 3-88: (N) Change the stance into Horse Stance (Ma Bu, 馬步) and swing the sword over the head and down to shoulder level. The sword points E. Inhale and exhale.

Figure 3-88A: The defender dodges an attack and then cuts the hand of the opponent.

31. The Bird Flying over the Waterfall (Tian Niao Fei Pu, 天鳥飛瀑)

Figure 3-89

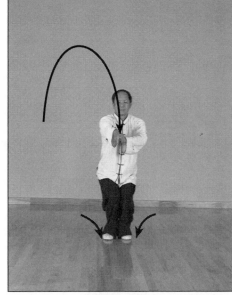

Figure 3-90

Figure 3-89A

Figure 3-90A

Figure 3-89: (N) Raise your right knee and swing the sword down on the right side of the leg. Inhale.

Figure 3-89A: The defender slides a low attack away.

Figure 3-90: (N) Step forward with your right leg and immediately follow with your left leg while swinging the sword up and then down. Exhale.

Figure 3-90A: The defender chops the sword down onto the opponent's head after the block.

32. Raise the Screen (Tiao Lian Shi, 挑簾勢)

Figure 3-91

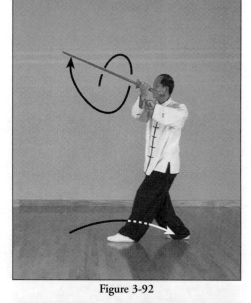

Figure 3-92

Figure 3-91A

Figure 3-92A

Figure 3-91: (E) Bring your right leg back so that the front of your body faces E. While moving back, slide the sword up to the E. Inhale.

Figure 3-91A: The defender steps the right leg back while sliding away a high attack.

Figure 3-92: (E) Circle the tip of the sword clockwise and slide upward and to the left. Exhale.

Figures 3-92A and 3-92B: After blocking, the defender circles the sword to

Figure 3-92B

the other side of the opponent's weapon and slides up the opponent's wrist. This movement can also be used as a block which slides an incoming attack to the left.

Figure 3-93: (E) Change the direction of the circle to counterclockwise. Circle to the left, down, and then up while lifting the left leg into The Golden Rooster Stands on One Leg Stance (Jin Ji Du Li, 金雞獨立). From the beginning of this posture until this movement, the sword has made a figure eight in front of the upper chest area. Inhale and then exhale.

Figure 3-93A: After blocking, the defender circles the sword to the right hand side of the opponent's weapon and slides upward to his fingers.

Figure 3-93

Figure 3-93A

33. Left and Right Wheel Sword (Zuo You Che Lun Jian, 左右車輪劍)

Figure 3-94

Figure 3-95

Figure 3-94A

Figure 3-95A

Figure 3-94: (E) Step down with your left leg and turn it out so that the stance is Crossed Legs Stance (Zuo Pan Bu, 坐盤步). At the same time, swing the sword down and back. The left hand touches the right wrist. Inhale.

Figure 3-94A: The defender slides an attack away.

Figure 3-95: (E) Bring your right leg forward into Mountain Climbing Stance (Deng Shan Bu, 蹬山步) and slide the sword up and straight ahead. The right palm faces upward and the left hand points back. Exhale.

Figure 3-95A: The defender slides the sword up and then forward to stab the opponent's throat.

33. Left and Right Wheel Sword—*continued*

Figure 3-96

Figure 3-97

Figure 3-96A

Figure 3-97A

Figure 3-96: (E) Turn your body to your right and slide the sword down and back while turning the blade until the right palm faces your body. Inhale.

Figure 3-96A: As the opponent attacks the lower body, the defender guides his weapon away.

34. The Swallow Picks Up Mud with Its Beak (Yan Zi Xian Ni, 燕子啣泥)

Figure 3-97: (E) Swing the sword back, up, and forward while stepping straight ahead with your left leg. Next, bring your right leg forward so both legs are together. Squat down. Exhale.

Figure 3-97A: After blocking in Figure 3-96A, the defender steps forward to counterattack over the top.

35. The Roc Spreads Its Wings (Da Peng Zhan Chi, 大鵬展翅)

Figure 3-98: (SW) Move your right leg back and turn the body clockwise to the SW. Swing the sword up diagonally while keeping your left hand on the right wrist. The stance is Mountain Climbing Stance (Deng Shan Bu, 蹬山步). Inhale and exhale.

Figure 3-98A: The defender dodges an attack and then cuts the opponent's wrist.

Figure 3-98

Figure 3-98A

36. Pick Up the Moon from the Sea Bottom (Hai Di Lao Yue, 海底撈月)

Figure 3-99

Figure 3-100

Figure 3-100A

Figure 3-99: (E) Turn the body counterclockwise to face E while swinging your left hand in front of your face. The sword stays behind. Inhale.

Figure 3-100: (E) Move your right leg forward into Mountain Climbing Stance (Deng Shan Bu, 蹬山步) and swing the sword down at knee level; your upper body leans forward. The left hand extends up and back. Exhale.

Figure 3-100A: This is a long range attack by the defender. After pushing the rod away, the defender leans forward to cut the opponent's knee. Naturally, the left hand can grab the opponent's long weapon to prevent him from further attack while you are cutting his knee.

37. Hold the Moon against the Chest (Huai Zhong Bao Yue, 懷中抱月)

Figure 3-101

Figure 3-102

Figure 3-101A

Figure 3-102A

Figure 3-101: (N) Pull the right leg in into False Stance (Xu Bu, 虛步) while drawing the sword back to your chest area. The body faces N while the sword is pointing to the E. Inhale.

Figure 3-101A: The defender slides away an attack to his face with the middle section of his sword.

38. The Night Demon Gauges the Depth of the Sea (Ye Cha Tan Hai, 夜叉探海)

Figure 3-102: (N) Step your right leg half a step to the right, and raise your left knee and slide downward toward N. Your upper body leans forward slightly and your left hand extends back. Exhale.

Figure 3-102A: After sliding the attack away, the defender steps to the opponent's left hand side while cutting down to the opponent's wrist.

39. The Rhino Looks at the Moon (Xi Niu Wang Yue, 犀牛望月)

Figure 3-103

Figure 3-104

Figure 3-103A

Figure 3-104A

Figure 3-103: (NW) Step your left leg down and face the NW while blocking upward with your sword, right palm facing in. Begin to inhale.

Figure 3-103A: The defender uses his sword to intercept an incoming attack.

40. Shoot the Geese (She Yan Shi, 射雁势)

Figure 3-104: (NW) Step your right leg half of a step forward and immediately step your left leg into False Stance (Xu Bu, 虚步). While you are doing so, you also circle your sword down to your right hand side, beside the right knee, and extend your left sword secret hand forward. Complete inhalation.

Figure 3-104A: After the defender has intercepted an incoming attack, he steps forward and uses his left hand to attack the opponent's chest. If the opponent's steps back to avoid the attack, the defender can use the next movement to step forward and stab his opponent's lower body.

41. The Blue Dragon Waves Its Claws (Qing Long Tan Zhua, 青龍探爪)

Figure 3-105

Figure 3-106

Figure 3-105: (NW) Step your left leg half a step forward and immediately step your right leg to the side to the left leg while also stabbing your sword forward and slightly downward. Exhale.

42. The Phoenix Spreads Its Wings (Feng Huang Shuang Zhan Chi, 鳳凰雙展翅)

Figure 3-106: (SE) Step the right leg back and turn your body 180 degrees clockwise while swinging your sword backward diagonally. Inhale and exhale.

43. Left and Right Step over Obstacle (Zuo You Kua Lan, 左右跨攔)

Figure 3-107

Figure 3-108

Figure 3-107A

Figure 3-108A

Figure 3-107: (E) Move your left leg in to the side of your right leg while moving the sword down to your left. Start to inhale.

Figure 3-107A: The defender uses the lower part of the sword to guide an attack away.

Figure 3-108: (E) Raise your left foot up to waist height and then push to the left. Complete inhalation.

Figure 3-108A: After the blocking, the defender uses the side of his left foot to push the opponent's weapon away.

43. Left and Right Step over Obstacle—*continued*

Figure 3-109

Figure 3-110

Figure 3-109A

Figure 3-110A

Figure 3-109: (E) Step your left leg down to NE while circling your sword and horizontally sliding it to the left. Exhale.

Figure 3-109A: The defender steps his left foot down and uses his sword to cut the opponent's waist.

Figure 3-110: (E) Move your right leg in to the side of the left leg while blocking the sword to the right. Start to inhale.

Figure 3-110A: The defender moves his right leg in while using the sword to block an incoming attack to his right.

Figure 3-111

Figure 3-112

Figure 3-111A

Figure 3-112A

Figure 3-111: (E) Lift your right leg and use the side of your right foot to push to the right. Complete inhalation.

Figure 3-111A: The defender uses the side of his right foot to push the opponent's weapon to his right.

Figure 3-112: (E) Step your right leg down to the SE while circling your sword to the left, down, and then sliding to the right. Exhale.

Figure 3-112A: The defender steps his right leg down and slides the right side of the opponent's waist.

44. Shoot the Geese (She Yan Shi, 射雁勢)

Figure 3-113

Figure 3-114

Figure 3-113A

Figure 3-113: (E) Shift your weight to your left foot while circling your sword up to the left of your upper chest. Start to inhale.

Figure 3-113A: The defender blocks an incoming attack to his left.

Figure 3-114: (E) Step your left leg to the E while circling your sword down. Complete inhalation.

Figure 3-115

Figure 3-116

Figure 3-115A

Figure 3-116A

Figure 3-115: (E) Step your left leg forward into False Stance (Xu Bu, 虛步), continue circling your sword to your right while extending your left hand sword secret forward. Exhale.

Figure 3-115A: After blocking, the defender steps forward and uses his left sword secret to attack the opponent's throat.

45. The White Ape Offers Fruit (Bai Yuan Xian Guo, 白猿獻果)

Figure 3-116: (E) Step your right leg forward while extending your sword forward. Inhale and exhale.

Figure 3-116A: In the last technique, if the opponent steps back to avoid the attack, the defender immediately steps his right leg forward and stabs the opponent's stomach.

46. Falling Flowers Posture (Luo Hua Shi, 落花勢)

Figure 3-117

Figure 3-118

Figure 3-117A

Figure 3-118A

Figure 3-117: (E) Turn your body to your left while circling the tip of your sword up. Inhale.

Figure 3-117A: The defender circles his sword up to his left to intercept an incoming attack.

Figure 3-118: (E) Step your right leg backward while circling the tip of the sword upward and to the right. Exhale.

Figure 3-118A: After blocking, the defender circles the sword down and then up to the right diagonally to cut the right side of the opponent's upper chest.

Figure 3-119

Figure 3-120

Figure 3-119A

Figure 3-120A

Figure 3-119: (E) Continue to circle the tip of your sword up to the right. Inhale.

Figure 3-119A: The defender blocks his sword up and to the right to intercept an incoming attack.

Figure 3-120: (E) Step your left leg backward while circling the tip of the sword upward and to your left. Exhale.

Figure 3-120A: After blocking, the defender circles the sword up and to his left diagonally to cut the opponent's underarm area.

Figure 3-121

Figure 3-122

Figures 3-121 to 3-123: (E) Repeat Figures 3-118 to 3-120 and then again Figure 3-119. In total there are five backward steppings and two and one-half figure eight tip circlings right in front of the face.

Figure 3-123

47. The Fair Lady Weaves with the Shuttle (Yu Nu Chuan Suo, 玉女穿梭)

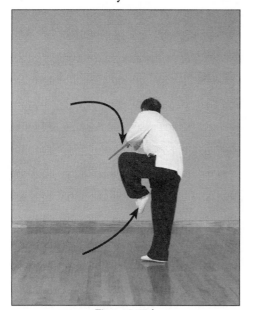

Figure 3-124

Figure 3-125

Figure 3-124A

Figure 3-126

Figure 3-124: (S) Raise your left knee and turn your body S while swinging the sword down. Exhale.

Figure 3-124A: The defender uses the sword to chop down on the opponent's wrist.

Figure 3-125: (S) Set your left leg down and turn N. Turn the sword in so that the blade points N. Inhale.

Figure 3-126: (N) Shift the stance to Mountain Climbing Stance (Deng Shan Bu, 蹬山步) and extend the sword forward and down. Exhale.

48. The White Tiger Waves Its Tail (Bai Hu Jiao Wei, 白虎攪尾)

Figure 3-127

Figure 3-128

Figure 3-127: (S) Turn your body 180 degrees clockwise to face S while swinging the sword diagonally up toward the S. Inhale and Exhale.

Figure 3-128: (E) Turn your body 90 degrees counterclockwise to face E while swinging your sword horizontally to the E. Inhale.

Figure 3-128A: The defender uses his left hand to grab the incoming long weapon attack while sliding his sword to the opponent's neck.

Figure 3-128A

Figure 3-129: (E) Step your right leg forward into False Stance (Xu Bu, 虛步) while bringing both of your hands to the middle chest area. Exhale.

Figure 3-129A: If the opponent's neck is too far away beyond reach, the defender immediately slides the sword back to the opponent's wrist.

Figure 3-129

Figure 3-129A

49. The Fish Jumps into the Dragon Gate (Yu Tiao Long Men, 魚跳龍門)

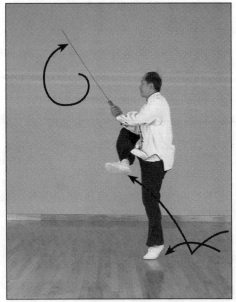

Figure 3-130   Figure 3-131

Figure 3-130: (E) Lift the right leg up, step forward and spring upward and jump forward while circling the sword in front of the body. Inhale.

Figure 3-131:(E) Step the right leg down into Mountain Climbing Stance (Deng Shan Bu, 蹬山步) and extend your sword forward.

50. The Black Dragon Wraps around the Post (Wu Long Jiao Zhu, 烏龍絞柱)

Figure 3-132

Figure 3-133

Figure 3-132A

Figure 3-133A

Figure 3-132: (E) Shift your weight back and enter Four-Six Stance (Si Liu Bu, 四六步) while sliding your sword to your left. Inhale.

Figure 3-132A: The defender blocks an incoming attack to his left while sitting back.

Figure 3-133: (E) Step your left leg forward while circling your sword to the back and then up on the left hand side of your body. Start to exhale.

Figure 3-133A: The defender steps his left leg forward and at the same time slides his sword to the opponent's upper chest.

50. The Black Dragon Wraps around the Post—*continued*

Figure 3-134

Figure 3-135

Figure 3-134A

Figure 3-135A

Figure 3-134: (SW) Turn your body 135 degrees clockwise while shifting the stance to Mountain Climbing Stance (Deng Shan Bu, 蹬山步), right leg forward, and swinging the sword straight down. Complete exhalation.

Figure 3-134A: The defender dodges an attack from behind and cuts the opponent's wrist.

Figure 3-135: (SW) Turn the sword in, bring your left hand to the right wrist and face E. Inhale.

Figure 3-135A: As an opponent attacks with a long weapon, the defender grabs the weapon with the left hand.

Figure 3-136: (E) Step forward with your right leg into Mountain Climbing Stance (Deng Shan Bu, 蹬山步) and extend the sword forward and down. Exhale.

Figure 3-136A: The defender moves in to stab the opponent.

Figure 3-136

Figure 3-136A

51. The Fairy Shows the Way—2 (Xian Ren Chi Lu-2, 仙人指路二)

Figure 3-137: (E) Sit back in Four-Six Stance (Si Liu Bu, 四六步) and slide the sword back to the left side. Your right palm faces in and your left hand touches the right wrist. Inhale.

Figure 3-137A: The defender pushes an attack away.

Figure 3-137

Figure 3-137A

52. Wind Blows Away the Plum Flowers (Feng Sao Mei Hua, 風掃梅花)

Figure 3-138

Figure 3-139

Figure 3-138A

Figures 3-138 and 3-139: (N) Spin 360 degrees clockwise on the toes of your right leg while extending both arms straight out. Exhale.

Figure 3-138A: After blocking, the defender cuts the opponent's throat.

52. Wind Blows Away the Plum Flowers—*continued*

Figure 3-140

Figure 3-141

Figure 3-141A

Figure 3-142

Figures 3-140 to 3-142: (N) Set your left leg down while circling the sword above your face. Look up. Inhale.

Figure 3-141A: The defender circles the sword in front of the face and leads the head back to neutralize an attack.

53. To Hold a Tablet (Shou Peng Ya Hu, 手捧牙笏)

Figure 3-143

Figure 3-144

Figure 3-143: (N) Step your left leg forward while holding the sword with the tip facing forward in front of your chest. Start to exhale.

Figure 3-144: (N) Follow with the right leg's forward stepping and at the same time stab your sword forward. Complete exhalation.

Figure 3-144A: After blocking, the defender moves in to stab the opponent in the neck.

Figure 3-144A

54. Hold the Sword and Return to the Original Stance (Bao Jian Gui Yuan, 抱劍歸元)

Figure 3-145

Figure 3-146

Figure 3-147

Figure 3-148

Figure 3-145: (N) Circle the sword down and then up, and touch the handle of the sword with the left hand to prepare it to take the sword. Begin to inhale.

Figure 3-146: (N) The left hand takes over the sword at the handle and turns the sword upside down. Continue to inhale.

Figure 3-147: (N) Continue the left hand's downward motion while opening the right arm. Continue to inhale.

Figure 3-148: (N) Step your left leg back while moving your right hand up to the right side of the ear. Continue to inhale.

Figure 3-149

Figure 3-150

Figure 3-149: (N) Step your right leg back and assume Horse Stance (Ma Bu, 馬步). Complete inhalation.

Figure 3-150: (N) Stand up while lowering your left hand. Exhale.

After you have completed the entire sequence, you should continue to keep your mind calm, breathing smoothly and uniformly for a couple of minutes.

Reference

1. 師父引進門，修行在自身。

CHAPTER 4

Taiji Sword Matching Practice 太極劍基本對練

4-1. INTRODUCTION 介紹

After the Taiji martial artist has learned the narrow blade sword sequence, he/she will go on to exercises that serve the same function as pushing hands, but which are done with a sword. These drills are called fighting forms or matching drills. The Taiji student must practice and become proficient in the fighting forms because he/she will train all the important abilities needed for free fighting: smooth Qi flow into the sword, fluid and lively movement, an understanding of the opponent's power, an ability to adhere, expertise in sword techniques, and proper defense. In this book, ten sword fighting forms will be shown and explained: six left neutralization and right side attack, and four right neutralization and left side attack. Later, experienced Taiji practitioners can develop their own fighting forms. Once all the requirements are met, the student proceeds to unrestricted fighting.

4-2. MATCHING PRACTICE 對練

In this section, we will introduce some examples of Taiji sword matching practice. These examples are only to serve the purpose of highlighting. Once you have learned and mastered the entire Taiji sword solo sequence, you should try to pick up the movements inside the sequence and create some other fighting matching sets. Remember, without practicing with a partner, you will never build up a correct feeling, and learn how to handle different situations. When you practice, you and your partner should start with wooden swords first. Only until you have mastered the skills should you use real swords for practice.

As usual, for ease of reference, the performer in the white pants shall be referred to as W, while the performer in the black pants shall be referred to as B.

Taiji Sword Matching Practice

Matching Practice #1
Coil Left and Stab Horizontally (Zuo Chan Ping Ci, 左纏平刺)

Figure 4-1

Figure 4-2

Figure 4-1: W steps forward and stabs B's throat (Figure 4-1). B steps backward and uses his sword to block and neutralize W's sword to his left.

Figure 4-2: B then coils his sword downward to stick with W's sword to open W's upper body and immediately steps forward to stab W's throat. Right before B's sword reaches the halfway point of attack, W steps back and blocks his sword to his left and neutralizes B's attack.

Figure 4-3

Figure 4-3. Repeat Figure 4-1. Continue the practice until the matching becomes natural and comfortable.

Matching Practice #2
Left Neutralizing and Stab Forward (Zuo Hua Qian Ci, 左化前刺)

Figure 4-4

Figure 4-5

Figure 4-6

This matching is very similar to the previous one but adds stepping to the right.

Figure 4-4: W steps his right leg forward and uses his sword to stab B's throat. B moves his left leg in to the side of his right leg while using his sword to block W's attack.

Figure 4-5: B steps to his right while stabbing his sword to W's throat. W steps his left leg in to the side of his right leg and uses his sword to block an incoming attack.

Figure 4-6: Repeat Figure 4-4. Continue the practice until the stepping and the matching become natural and comfortable.

Matching Practice #3
Left Neutralize and Right Stab (Zuo Hua You Ci, 左化右刺)

Figure 4-7

Figure 4-8

Figure 4-9

This matching again is very similar to the previous one except this time B stabs to W's chest with the sword blade vertical. The blocking is lower and the neutralization is slightly different from the previous set.

Figure 4-7: W stabs at B's stomach area. B slides the attack away to his left while stepping his left leg to the side of his right leg.

Figure 4-8: B steps to the side with his right leg and stabs at B's stomach area. W moves his left leg in to the side of his right leg while using his sword to neutralize B's attack to his left.

Figure 4-9: Repeat Figure 4-7. Continue the practice until the stepping and the matching become natural and comfortable.

Matching Practice #4
Left Neutralize and Right Pull (Zuo Hua You Dan, 左化右带)

Figure 4-10

Figure 4-11

Figure 4-10: W steps his right leg to his right and at the same time uses the sword to cut at B's neck with a horizontal slash. B dodges the attack by turning his body to the left slightly, stepping his left leg in to the side of his right leg while using his sword to stick with the incoming sword and lead it to his left.

Figure 4-11: B steps his right leg to his right and uses his sword to slide W's neck. W turns his body to his left

Figure 4-12

slightly, steps his left leg in to the side of his right leg, while using his sword to stick with an incoming attack and lead it to his left hand side.

Figure 4-12: Repeat Figure 4-10. Continue the practice until the stepping and the matching become natural and comfortable.

Matching Practice #5
Left Whirlwind (Zuo Xuan Feng, 左旋風)

This is a mutual wrist cut chasing practice (wrist coiling training) between both B and W. First practice stationary, until both sides are smooth and natural. Only then should you advance to the stepping practice.

Figures 4-13 and 4-14: Both B and W start by facing each other. W circles the tip section of the sword clockwise and tries to cut B's wrist. B circles his wrist away from cutting while also using the tip section of his sword to try to cut W's wrist with a clockwise circular motion. Though both B and W's swords chase each other's wrist, neither one should actually cut the other. You should practice slowly at first, until it becomes smooth and natural, then you should speed up the practice.

Matching Practice #5
Left Whirlwind—*continued*

Figure 4-13

Figure 4-14

Figure 4-15

Figure 4-16

Figure 4-15: After you have mastered the stationary practice, you should then add the stepping into the practice. First, you start the same wrist circling practice while facing each other.

Figure 4-16: Next, when B cuts down W's wrist, he steps his right leg to cross his left leg. In order to avoid the cut, W continues his circling with B while also stepping his right leg right in front of his left leg.

Figure 4-17

Figure 4-17: When B loses his target, he steps his left leg to the side again to set up the best angle for attack and at the same time uses his sword to cut W's wrist again. Naturally, in order to avoid the cut, W also steps his left leg to his left while continuing his sword circling. You should repeat the practice. Eventually, both you and your partner will be stepping in a circle.

Matching Practice #6
Left Neutralize and File the Wrist (Zuo Hua Cuo Wan, 左化銼腕)

Figure 4-18

Figure 4-19

Figure 4-18: W steps his right leg forward and uses his sword to stab B's abdominal area. B withdraws his right leg while using his sword to block and neutralize the attack to the left.

Figure 4-19: B steps with his front leg to the side and slides his left leg to follow the stepping, while also filing down with his sword onto W's wrist. W immediately steps his right leg in, and turns his body to his left slightly, while using his sword to block and neutralize B's attack to his left.

Figure 4-20

Figure 4-20: Repeat Figure 4-18 except W will attack B's wrist by filing this time instead of stabbing the abdominal area.

Matching Practice #7
Right Whirlwind (You Xuan Feng, 右旋風)

This training is the same as Matching Practice #5, except that the circling direction for both W and B are reversed from that of #5.

Figures 4-21 and 4-22: Again, both B and W are facing each other and using the tip section of the sword to chase each other's wrist. B circles his wrist and sword tip clockwise, while W circles his wrist and sword tip counterclockwise. Again, both you and your partner should practice slowly at first until it becomes smooth and natural. Then you should speed up or go to the following stepping routine.

Matching Practice #7
Right Whirlwind—*continued*

Figure 4-21

Figure 4-22

Figure 4-23

Figure 4-24

Figure 4-23: Again start the practice with stationary circling.

Figure 4-24: B steps his left leg to cross his right leg while using his sword to circle and slide W's wrist. In order to avoid the cut, W also steps his left leg across his right leg while continuing his sword circling.

Figure 4-25: B steps his right leg to his right and again uses his sword to cut W's wrist. W also steps his right leg to readjust his position while continuing the

Figure 4-25

sword's circling to avoid the cut. Repeat the same practice continuously. Eventually, both you and your partner will be stepping in a counterclockwise direction.

Matching Practice #8
Right Neutralize and Downward Stab (You Hua Xia Ci, 右化下刺)

Figure 4-26

Figure 4-27

Figure 4-26: W steps his right leg forward while using his sword to stab B's abdominal area. B immediately draws his right leg in while using his sword to block and push an incoming attack to the right.

Figure 4-27: After blocking, B steps his right leg forward and stabs his sword forward and down at W's abdominal area. W then steps his right leg back and at the same time slides his sword back to dissolve B's attack.

Figure 4-28: W attacks to renew the cycle.

Figure 4-28

Matching Practice #9
Right Neutralize and Left Pull (You Hua Zuo Dai, 右化左帶)

Figure 4-29

Figure 4-30

Figure 4-31

Figure 4-29: W steps his left leg to his left and uses his sword to cut B's neck. B steps his right leg across his left leg and uses his sword to block and slide the attack away, slightly up and to his right, to neutralize the attack.

Figure 4-30: B immediately coils his sword down and steps his left leg to his left while sliding his sword to W's neck. B crosses his right leg right in front of his left leg while turning his body slightly to his right, and using his sword to block and slide an incoming attack to his right and up slightly.

Figure 4-31: Repeat Figure 4-29 to renew the cycle.

Matching Practice #10
Cloud Above the Head and Stab Forward (Shang Yun Qian Ci, 上雲前刺)

Figure 4-32

Figure 4-33

Figure 4-34

Figure 4-35

Figure 4-32: W steps both of his legs forward and uses his sword to stab B's throat. B steps both of his legs back to maintain distance while circling his sword clockwise in front of and slightly above his head to intercept and neutralize an incoming attack.

Figure 4-33: After the neutralization, B continues to press his sword down to open W's head area.

Figure 4-34: Immediately, B steps both of his legs forward and uses his

Figure 4-36

sword to stab W's throat. In order to avoid the attack, W steps both of his legs back while circling his sword in front of and slightly above his head to neutralize B's stabbing.

Figure 4-35: After the neutralization, W continues to circle his sword down to press B's sword down, to open B's head area for further attack.

Figure 4-36: Repeat Figure 4-32 to renew the cycle.

CHAPTER 5

Conclusion 結論

As mentioned at the beginning of this book, there are many different Taiji styles in existence today, after more than one thousand years of development. Therefore, there are also many different versions of Taiji sword training. However, it does not matter how the branches and flowers grow, they all originated from the same Taiji root (i.e., Yin and Yang theory). Therefore, when you practice Taijiquan or Taiji sword, you should not forget the basic theory upon which all Taiji styles have built.

The Taiji sword introduced in this book can only offer you a concept. It remains only a branch of a big Taiji tree. If you wish to study deeper, you should keep your eyes open and continue your learning from other sources. Only from different perspectives can your perception and judgment grow deeper and more accurate. In fact, since all of the sword techniques were created based on the structure of the sword, and similar strategic movements, almost all of the different styles (both internal and external) have the same sword root. When this sword root combines with Taiji theory, the Taiji sword techniques are created. Therefore, it would be wise if you were to also learn and practice some external sword skills. This will significantly enhance your understanding of the uses of the sword.

Although this book offers you both training theory and pictures, often it is not easy to figure out the correct movements from photos, especially moves meant to be performed in a continuous stream. Therefore, if possible, you should also obtain a videotape. From the videotape, you will be able to see the accurate connecting movements. Often, these connecting movements are the key movements to the flow of techniques.

You should also recognize the fact that even if you have the videotape, you will still lose the feeling of the practice. The accurate feeling of the art can usually only be obtained from many years of accurate practice. Normally, a qualified master can lead you to a deep, profound feeling in a short time. If possible, you should also take some seminars or private lessons from a qualified master. From a master, you will not only be able to refine your movements, but you will also get the most important factor for learning the sword. This most important factor is the *feeling, or the inner quality of the art.* In many ways, the quality of your practice is as important as the quantity. Without this deep accurate feeling, the art you learn will be a shadow.

Names of Taiji Sword Techniques

YANG'S TAIJI SWORD SEQUENCE 楊氏太極劍

1. Beginning (Qi Shi) 起勢, p. 103.

2. Step Forward and Close with Sword (Shang Bu He Jian Shi) 上步合劍勢, p. 104.

3. The Fairy Shows the Way-1 (Xian Ren Zhi Lu-1) 仙人指路一, p. 105.

4. Three Rings Envelop the Moon (San Huan Tao Yue) 三環套月, p. 106.

5. Big Chief Star (Da Kui Xing) 大魁星, p. 108.

6. The Swallow Dips Its Beak in the Water (Yan Zi Chao Shui) 燕子抄水, p. 110.

7. Left Sweep, Right Sweep (Zuo You Lan Sao) 左右攔掃, p. 111.

8. Little Chief Star (Xiao Kui Xing) 小魁星, p. 113.

9. The Yellow Bee Enters the Hole (Huang Feng Ru Dong) 黃蜂入洞, p. 115.

10. The Spirit Cat Catches the Mouse (Ling Mao Bu Shu) 靈貓捕鼠, p. 116.

11. The Dragonfly Touches the Water (Qing Ting Tian Shui) 蜻蜓點水, p. 118.

12. The Swallow Enters the Nest (Yan Zi Ru Chao) 燕子入巢, p. 119.

13. The Phoenix Spreads Its Wings (Feng Huang Shuang Zhan 鳳凰雙展翅, p. 121.

14. Right Whirlwind (You Xuan Feng) 右旋風, p. 122.

15. Little Chief Star (Xiao Kui Xing) 小魁星, p. 124.

16. Left Whirlwind (Zuo Xuan Feng) 左旋風, p. 125.

17. Waiting for a Fish (Deng Yu Shi) 等魚勢, p. 127.

18. Part the Grass in Search of Snake (Bo Cao Xun She) 撥草尋蛇, p. 128.

19. Hold the Moon against the Chest (Huai Zhong Bao Yue) 懷中抱月, p. 131.

20. Send the Bird to the Woods (Song Niao Shang Lin) 送鳥上林, p. 131.

21. Black Dragon Waves Its Tail (Wu Long Bai Wei) 烏龍襬尾, p. 132.

22. The Wind Blows the Lotus Leaf (Feng Juan He Ye) 風捲荷葉, p. 133.

23. The Lion Shakes Its Head (Shi Zi Yao Tou) 獅子搖頭, p. 135.

24. The Tiger Holds Its Head (Hu Bao Tou) 虎抱頭, p. 138.

25. The Wild Horse Jumps the Stream (Ye Ma Tiao Jian) 野馬跳澗, p. 139.

26. Turn Body and Rein In the Horse (Fan Shen Le Ma) 翻身勒馬, p. 140.

27. Compass (Zhi Nan Zhen) 指南針, p. 141.

28. Clean Up Dust In the Wind (Ying Feng Dan Chen) 迎風撣塵, p. 142.

29. Push the Boat With the Current (Shun Shui Tui Zhou) 順水推舟, p. 145.

30. The Shooting Star Chasing the Moon (Liu Xing Gan Yue) 流星趕月, p. 146.

31. The Bird Flying Over the Waterfall (Tian Niao Fei Pu) 天鳥飛瀑, p. 147.

32. Raise the Screen (Tiao Lian Shi) 挑簾勢, p. 148.

33. Left and Right Wheel Sword (Zuo You Che Lun Jian) 左右車輪劍, p. 150.

34. The Swallow Picks Up Mud with Its Beak (Yan Zi Xian Ni) 燕子啣泥, p. 151.

35. The Roc Spreads Its Wings (Da Peng Zhan Chi) 大鵬展翅, p. 152.

36. Pick Up the Moon from the Sea Bottom (Hai Di Lao Yue) 海底撈月, p. 153.

37. Hold the Moon against the Chest (Huai Zhong Bao Yue) 懷中抱月, p. 154.

38. The Night Demon Gauges the Depth of the Sea (Ye Cha Tan Hai) 夜叉探海, p. 154.

39. The Rhino Looks at the Moon (Xi Niu Wang Yue) 犀牛望月, p. 155.

40. Shoot the Geese (She Yan Shi) 射雁勢, p. 155.

41. The Blue Dragon Waves Its Claws (Qing Long Tan Zhua) 青龍探爪, p. 156.

42. The Phoenix Spreads Its Wings (Feng Huang Shuang Zhan Chi) 鳳凰雙展翅, p. 156.

43. Left and Right Step over Obstacle (Zuo You Kua Lan) 左右跨攔, p. 157.

44. Shoot the Geese (She Yan Shi) 射雁勢, p. 160.

45. The White Ape Offers Fruit (Bai Yuan Xian Guo) 白猿獻果, p. 161.

46. Falling Flowers Posture (Luo Hua Shi) 落花勢, p. 162.

47. The Fair Lady Weaves with the Shuttle (Yu Nu Chuan Suo) 玉女穿梭, p. 165.

48. The White Tiger Waves Its Tail (Bai Hu Jiao Wei) 白虎攪尾, p. 166.

49. The Fish Jumps into the Dragon Gate (Yu Tiao Long Men) 魚跳龍門, p. 168.

50. The Black Dragon Wraps around the Post (Wu Long Jiao Zhu) 烏龍絞柱, p. 169.

51. Fairy Shows the Way—2 (Xian Ren Chi Lu-2) 仙人指路二, p. 172.

52. Wind Blows Away the Plum Flowers (Feng Sao Mei Hua) 風掃梅花, p. 173.

53. To Hold a Tablet (Shou Peng Ya Hu) 手捧牙笏, p. 175.

54. Hold the Sword and Return to the Original Stance (Bao Jian Gui Yuan) 抱劍歸元, p. 176.

Translation and Glossary of Chinese Terms

Ba 拔
Draw back or pull. One of the basic sword techniques.

Bai He 白鶴
Means "White Crane." One of the southern Chinese martial styles.

Bao 抱
Embrace. One of the basic sword techniques.

Bei Zhou (557-581 A.D.) 北周
Northern Zhou Dynasty. One of the dynasties in Chinese history.

Beng 崩
Sink or collapse. One of the basic sword techniques.

Bi Shou 匕首
Dagger.

Cao-Cao 曹操
The ruler of Wei. Wei was one of the three kingdoms in The Three Kingdoms Dynasty which followed the Han Dynasty and lasted 60 years (220-280 A.D.).

Chan 纏
Wrap. One of the basic sword techniques.

Chang Chuan (Changquan) 長拳
Means "Long Range Fist." Chang Chuan includes all northern Chinese long range martial styles.

Chang Jiang (Yangtze River) 長江(揚子江)
Literally, long river. Refers to the Yangtze river in southern China.

Chang Sui Jian 長繐劍
Any sword with long tassels. Commonly used in northern styles.

Changquan (Chang Chuan) 長拳
Means "Long Range Fist." Changquan includes all northern Chinese long range martial styles.

Cheng, Gin-Gsao 曾金灶
Dr. Yang, Jwing-Ming's White Crane master.

Chi Kung (Qigong) 氣功
The Gongfu of Qi, which means the study of Qi.

Chi You 蚩尤
The opponent of the Yellow Emperor (Huang Di) during the years 2697-2597 B.C.

Chin Na (Qin Na) 擒拿
Literally means "grab control." A component of Chinese martial arts which emphasizes grabbing techniques, to control your opponent's joints, in conjunction with attacking certain acupuncture cavities.

Chong 沖
Thrust. One of the basic sword techniques.

Chong Mai 衝脈
Thrusting Vessel. One of the eight Qi vessels in Chinese medicine.

Chou 抽
Draw back or pull. One of the basic sword techniques.

Chuan 穿
Bore. One of the basic sword techniques.

Chun Qiu (722-484 B.C.) 春秋
The Spring and Autumn Period. One of the epochs in Chinese history.

Ci 刺
Stab. One of the basic sword techniques.

Cuo 銼、錯
File. One of the basic sword techniques.

Dai 帶
Draw back or pull. One of the basic sword techniques.

Deng Shan Bu 蹬山步
Mountain Climbing Stance. One of the basic stances in the northern styles of Chinese martial arts.

Dian 點
Point. One of the basic sword techniques.

Dian Xue Massages 點穴按摩
Chinese massage techniques in which the acupuncture cavities are stimulated through pressing. Dian Xue massage is also called acupressure, and is the root of Japanese Shiatsu.

Fa 划
Slide. One of the basic sword techniques.

Fan Li Ci 反立刺
Reverse vertical stab. One of the sword stabbing techniques.

Fan Liao 反撩
Reverse slide up. One of the sword sliding techniques.

Fan Ping Ci 反平刺
Reverse horizontal stab. One of the sword stabbing techniques.

Gai 蓋
Cover. One of the basic sword techniques.

Gan Jiang 干將
A very famous sword maker, who also named one of his best swords "Gan Jiang." His wife, Mo Xie was also a well-known sword maker at the time.

Gong (Kung) 功
Energy or hard work.

Ge 格
Impede or hamper. One of the basic sword techniques.

Gong Jian Bu 弓箭步
Bow and arrow stance, also called Mountain Climbing Stance. One of the basic stances in northern styles of Chinese martial arts.

Gongfu (Kung Fu) 功夫
Means "energy-time." Anything which will take time and energy to learn or to accomplish is called Gongfu.

Gu-Zheng 古箏
A stringed instrument, played by plucking, in some ways similar to the zither.

Gua 挂
Lift. One of the basic sword techniques.

Gua Wan 刮腕
Paring wrist. One of the basic sword techniques.

Han (206 B.C.-220 A.D.) 漢
A Dynasty in Chinese history.

Han Race 漢族
The major race in China.

Han, Ching-Tang 韓慶堂
A well known Chinese martial artist, especially in Taiwan in the last forty years. Master Han is also Dr. Yang, Jwing-Ming's Long Fist Grand Master.

He Lu 闔閭
A Wu emperor who loved collecting swords.

Henan 河南省
The province in China where the Shaolin Temple is located.

Heng 橫
Side Cut. One of the basic sword techniques.

Himalayans 喜馬拉亞人
The native residents of the Himalaya mountain range.

Huai Nan Wan Hua Shu 淮南萬華術
Huai Nan's Thousand Crafts. The name of a book.

Huang Di (2690-2590 B.C.) 黃帝
Huang Di, called the "Yellow Emperor" because he occupied the territory near the Yellow River.

Hubei Province 湖北省
One of the provinces in China.

Huo 豁
Expand. One of the basic sword techniques.

Jia 架
Block. One of the basic sword techniques.

Jian 劍
Straight sword.

Jian 剪
Clip. One of the basic sword techniques.

Jian Chi 劍池
Sword Pond. Located in Suzhou of Jiangsu Province.

Jian Jue 劍訣
The secret sword. The hand posture in which the index and middle fingers are straight, while the other three fingers are held to touch the center of the palm.

Jian Ke 劍客
In ancient times, the name commonly given to a person who had mastered the sword.

Jian Qiao 劍鞘
The sheath.

Jian Sui 劍繐
The tassel.

Jiao 絞
Entwine. One of the basic sword techniques.

Jie 截
Intercept. One of the basic sword techniques.

Jie 揭
Rise. One of the basic sword techniques.

Jin 金
The Mongols. The race of people called Mongols is also called Jin.

Jin Ji Du Li 金雞獨立
Golden Rooster Stands On One Leg Stance. One of the stances commonly found in Chinese martial arts.

Jin, Shao-Feng 金紹峰
Dr. Yang, Jwing-Ming's White Crane grand master.

Ju Chi Jian 鋸齒劍
Saw toothed sword. This sword has a serrated edge to give it greater cutting ability. The edge design probably originated when someone found that a badly nicked blade seemed to cut more viciously. The two holes in the tip of the sword resemble the eyes of a snake, and make a whooshing noise when the sword is swung.

Ju Que 巨闕
One of the famous swords forged by Ou Ye Zi, during the Chinese Spring and Autumn Period (722-484 B.C.), and the Warring States Period (403-222 B.C.). It is said that this sword was so sharp that if dipped in water, it would be withdrawn perfectly dry.

Kan 砍
Chop. One of the basic sword techniques.

Kao Tao 高濤
Master Yang, Jwing-Ming's first Taijiquan master.

King Wen of Zhou 周文王
An emperor of the Chinese Zhou dynasty.

Kun Wu Jian 崑峿劍
The name of a sword sequence. Also commonly used to refer to the sword itself.

Kung 功
Means energy or hard work.

Kung Fu (Gongfu) 功夫
Means "energy-time." Anything which will take time and energy to learn or to accomplish is called Kung Fu.

La 拉
Draw back or pull. One of the basic sword techniques.

Lan 攔
Hinder or obstruct. One of the basic sword techniques.

Le 将
Draw back or pull. One of the basic sword techniques.

Li, Mao-Ching 李茂清
Dr. Yang, Jwing-Ming's Long Fist master.

Liao 撩
Slide upward. One of the sword sliding techniques.

Liu Bei 劉備
The ruler of Han. Han was one of the three kingdoms in The Three Kingdoms Dynasty.

Long Quan 龍泉
A county in Zhejiang Province which is well known for producing good weapons.

Long Quan Jian 龍泉劍
A name for a sword. Can also mean the swords produced in Long Quan county of Zhejiang Provinces.

Ma Bu 馬步
Horse Stance. One of the basic stances in northern Chinese martial arts.

Ming Dynasty (1368-1644 A.D.) 明朝
One of the dynasties in Chinese history.

Mo 抹、摸
Smear. One of the basic sword techniques.

Mo Xie 莫邪
A very famous sword maker, who named one of her best swords "Mo Xie." Her Husband, Gan Jiang was also a well-known sword maker at the time.

Mongolians 蒙古人

An Asian race living to the west of China. In ancient times they were very warlike and extremely efficient militarily.

Nei Cuo 內銼

Internal file. One of the sword's filing techniques.

Nei Gai 內蓋

Internal cover. One of the sword's covering techniques.

Nei Jiao 內絞

Internal wrap. One of the sword's wrapping techniques.

Nei Jie 內截

Internal intercept. One of the sword's intercepting techniques.

Nei Le 內捋

Internal draw back. One of the sword's drawing back techniques.

Nei Shang Tiao 內上挑

Internal pluck. One of the sword's plucking techniques.

Nei Xia Lan 內下攔

Low internal hinder. One of the sword's hindering techniques.

Nei Zhong Lan 內中攔

Internal hinder. One of the sword's hindering techniques.

Ou Ye Zi 歐冶子

One of the three most famous sword makers in the Chinese Spring and Autumn Period (722-484 B.C.) and the Warring States Period (403-222 B.C.). The other two well-known sword makers were Gan Jiang and Mo Xie. Ou Ye Zi forged two very famous swords, Ju Que and Zhan Lu.

Pao 拋

Swaying or throwing. One of the basic sword techniques.

Pi 劈

Split. One of the basic sword techniques.

Pu Yuan 蒲元

A famous sword maker during the Chinese Three Kingdoms Period (221-280 A.D.).

Qi (Chi) 氣

Chinese term for universal energy. A current popular model is that the Qi circulating in the human body is bioelectric in nature.

Qi, Ji-Guang 戚繼光

A well known general in the Ming Dynasty (1386-1644 A.D.).

Qi Men Jian 戚門劍

Qi's Family Sword. The name given to the many sword sequences created by Qi, Ji-Guang.

Qi Xing Jian 七星劍

Seven Star Sword. The name of a sword sequence. Also commonly used to refer to the sword itself.

Qigong (Chi Kung) 氣功
The Gongfu of Qi, which means the study of Qi.

Qin Dynasty (255-206 B.C.) 秦朝
One of the dynasties in Chinese history.

Qin Na (Chin Na) 擒拿
Literally means "grab control." A component of Chinese martial arts which emphasizes grabbing techniques to control your opponent's joints, in conjunction with attacking certain acupuncture cavities.

Qin Shi (221-209 B.C.) 秦始皇
An emperor of the Qin Dynasty (255-206 B.C.).

Qin Yang 沁陽
A county in Henan Province.

Qing Dynasty (1644-1911 A.D.) 清朝
One of the dynasties in Chinese history.

San Cai Jian 三才劍
Three Power Sword. Name of a sword sequence. Also commonly used to refer to the sword itself.

San Guo (220-280 A.D.) 三國
Three Kingdoms Period. A period during which China was divided into three kingdoms: Wei, Han, and Wu.

Sao 掃
Sweep. One of the basic sword techniques.

Shang Cuo 上銼
Upward file. One of the sword's filing techniques.

Shang Dynasty (1766-1122 B.C.) 商朝
Shang Nei Mo 上內抹
High internal smear. One of the sword's smearing techniques.

Shang Tuo 上托
Upward bear. One of the sword's bearing techniques.

Shang Wai Mo 上外抹
High external smear. One of the sword's smearing techniques.

Shaolin 少林
"Young woods." Name of the Shaolin Temple.

Shaolin Temple 少林寺
A monastery located in Henan Province, China. The Shaolin Temple is well known because of its martial arts training.

She She Jian 蛇舌劍
Snake tongue sword. This sword has a wavy blade, which makes for a fearful cut. It also has a forked point, that may have given the fighter a way to catch his opponent's weapon at long range.

Shi Xiang Zu 師襄子
Confucius' music teacher.

Shu 束
Bind. One of the basic sword techniques.

Shu 蜀

Sichuan Province is also called Shu.

Si Liu Bu 四六步

Four-Six Stance. One of the basic stances in northern Chinese martial styles.

Sichuan Province 四川省(蜀)

A province in western China.

Song Dynasty (960-1280 A.D.) 宋朝

One of the dynasties in Chinese history.

Sui and Tang Dynasties (581-907 A.D.) 隋、唐

Two of the dynasties in Chinese history.

Suzhou 蘇州

A city in Jiangsu Province.

Tai Chi Chuan (Taijiquan) 太極拳

A Chinese internal martial style which is based on the theory of Taiji (grand ultimate).

Taiji 太極

Means "grand ultimate." It is this force which generates two poles, Yin and Yang.

Taiji Jian 太極劍

A sword sequence practiced in Taijiquan. Taiji Jian also commonly refers to the sword.

Taijiquan (Tai Chi Chuan) 太極拳

A Chinese internal martial style which is based on the theory of Taiji (grand ultimate).

Taipei 台北

The capital city of Taiwan, located in the north.

Taiwan 台灣

An island to the south-east of mainland China. Also known as "Formosa."

Taiwan University 台灣大學

A well known university located in northern Taiwan.

Taizuquan 太祖拳

A style of Chinese external martial arts.

Tamkang 淡江

Name of a University in Taiwan.

Tamkang College Guoshu Club 淡江國術社

A Chinese martial arts club founded by Dr. Yang when he was studying in Tamkang College.

Tang Dynasty (618-907 A.D.) 唐朝

One of the dynasties in Chinese history.

Ti 提

Rise. One of the basic sword techniques.

Tiao 挑
Pluck. One of the basic sword techniques.

Tui Na 推拿
Push and grab. A Chinese Qigong massage technique for healing.

Tuo 托
Bear. One of the basic sword techniques.

Wai Cuo 外銼
External file. One of the sword's filing techniques.

Wai Gai 外蓋
External cover. One of the sword's covering techniques.

Wai Jiao 外絞
External wrap. One of the sword's wrapping techniques.

Wai Jie 外截
External intercept. One of the sword's intercepting techniques.

Wai Le 外捋
External draw back. One of the sword's drawing back techniques.

Wai Shang Tiao 外上挑
External pluck. One of the sword's plucking techniques.

Wai Xia Lan 外下攔
Low external hinder. One of the sword's hindering techniques.

Wai Zhong Lan 外中攔
External hinder. One of the sword's hindering techniques.

Wen Jian 文劍
Scholar sword. The scholar sword, also known as the female sword (Ci Jian), is lighter and shorter than the martial or male sword (Xiong Jian).

Wen Wang Cao 文王操
A piece of music composed by Wen Wang of Zhou.

Wilson Chen 陳威伸
Dr. Yang, Jwing-Ming's friend.

Wu 吳
One of the dynasties in Chinese history.

Wu Dai (907-960 A.D.) 五代
A period of Chinese history that includes five dynasties.

Wu Gou Jian 吳鉤劍
Wu hooked sword. This sword was invented during the Wu Dynasty (222-280 A.D.), and is designed for cutting an enemies' limbs, or his horses' legs, after blocking his weapon.

Wu Jian 武劍
Martial sword. The martial sword, also known as the male sword (Xiong Jian), is heavier and longer than the scholar or female sword (Ci Jian).

Wu Kang 武康
A county in Zhejiang Province known for the production of high quality ancient weapons.

Wudang Jian 武當劍
The sword techniques developed at Wudang mountain.

Wudang Mountain 武當山
A mountain located in Fubei Province in China.

Wuji 無極
No extremity. A state of no discrimination between Yin and Yang. Infinite smoothness.

Wushu (Gongfu) 武術(功夫)
Literally, martial technique. It is commonly called Guoshu (i.e., country techniques) in Taiwan or Gongfu in Western society.

Wuyi 武藝
Literally, "martial arts."

Xi 洗
Wash. One of the basic sword techniques.

Xia Wai Mo 下外抹
Low external smear. One of the sword's smearing techniques.

Xie Nei Mo 下內抹
Low internal smear. One of the sword's smearing techniques.

Xie Pi 斜劈
Diagonal chop. One of the sword's chopping techniques.

Xie Tuo 斜托
Diagonal bear. One of the sword's bearing techniques.

Xinzhu Xian 新竹縣
Birthplace of Dr. Yang, Jwing-Ming in Taiwan.

Xu Bu 虛步
False Stance, also called Tricky Stance. One of the basic stances in all Chinese martial styles.

Xuan Ji Bu 玄機步
Tricky Stance, also called False Stance. One of the basic stances in all Chinese martial styles.

Xue Gou 血溝
The blood groove. This is a groove on the sword blade that allows pressure to equalize on either side of a sword thrust into an opponent's body, permitting easy withdrawal.

Ya 壓
Press down. One of the basic sword techniques.

Yang, Jwing-Ming 楊俊敏
Author of this book.

Yangtze River (Chang Jiang) 揚子江（長江）
Also called Chang Jiang (i.e., long river). One of the two major rivers in China.

Yao 搖
Shake. One of the basic sword techniques.

Yi Jing 易經
Book of Changes. A book of divination written during the Zhou dynasty (1122-255 B.C.).

Yu Long 雨龍
Rain dragon. The name of a sword. Also called Judge Dee's sword.

Yuan Dynasty (1206-1368 A.D.) 元朝
One of the dynasties in Chinese history.

Yun 雲
Cloud. One of the basic sword techniques.

Zhan 斬
Cut. One of the basic sword techniques.

Zhan Guo (403-222 B.C.) 戰國
The Warring States Period. An epoch in Chinese history.

Zhan Lu 湛盧
One of the two famous swords made by sword maker Ou Ye Zi, during the Chinese Spring and Autumn Period (722-484 B.C.) and the Warring States Period (403-222 B.C.). The other sword was called "Ju Que."

Zhang, Xiang-San 張詳三
A well known Chinese martial artist in Taiwan.

Zhejiang Province 浙江省
A province of China near the south-east coast.

Zhen Dan Tian 真丹田
Real Dan Tian. Located approximately one inch below the navel and three inches inside the body.

Zheng Li Ci 正立刺
Vertical stab. One of the sword's stabbing techniques.

Zheng Liao 正撩
Normal slide up. One of the sword's sliding techniques.

Zheng Pi 正劈
Vertical chop. One of the sword's chopping techniques.

Zheng Ping 正平刺
Horizontal stab. One of the sword's stabbing techniques.

Zheng Tuo 正托
Upward bear. One of the sword's bearing techniques.

Zhou Dynasty (909-255 B.C.) 周朝
One of the dynasties in Chinese history.

Zhuo Lu 涿鹿
Location of an ancient battle between the Emperor Huang Di's forces and his opponent, Chi You.

Zuo Pan Bu 坐盤步
Crossed Legs Stance. One of the basic stances in northern Chinese martial styles.

Index

Accuracy Training, 32
Adhering, 18-19, 52-53, 80
Advance Forward File, 82
Applications, 19-21, 99-176, 206
Arc the Arms, 43-44
Axial Center, 80-81
Bamboo Twisting, 29
Barehand Taiji, 18
Basic Training, 17, 53, 81-96, 206
Big Chief Star, 108
Bind, 76, 198
Bioelectricity, 33
Block, 20, 77-78
Blood Groove, 15, 201
Bore, 9, 76, 193
Bow and Arrow Stance, 24, 194
Care of the Sword, 6
Carrying the Sword, 3
Cavities, 28, 35-36, 193, 198
Cavity Press, 21
Chan, 41, 46, 69, 179, 192
Chop, 54, 59, 101, 165, 196, 201-202
Chuan, 76, 165
Clean Up Dust in the Wind, 92, 142, 144
Clip, 78, 195
Cloud, 72, 188, 202
Cloud Above the Head and Stab Forward,
    188
Coil and Turn, 41-42, 46
Coil Left and Stab Horizontally, 179
Coiling, 18-19, 32-33, 41, 46, 52-53, 80,
    182
Compass, 102, 141
Confucius, 100-101, 198
Cover, 73, 193, 197, 200
Cut, 77
Dan Tian, 26, 28, 34-38, 103, 202
Defensive Attack, 20
Dodging, 21
Draw Back, 62, 192-193, 196-197, 200
Embrace, 75, 192
EMF (Electro-Motive Force), 24-27
Entwine, 69, 195
Essence, 18, 26, 28, 33, 53, 100-101, 206
Expand, 34, 39-40, 64, 195
Expand the Bow, 39-40
External, 17, 19, 24, 27-28, 37, 59, 61-62,
    66-69, 71, 73, 189, 198-201

External Styles, 19, 24, 28
Fairy Points the Way, 50, 52
Falling Flowers Posture, 96, 162
False Stance, 26
File, 68, 82, 184, 193, 197-198, 200
Forward and Backward Coil, 46
Foundation, 2, 7, 17-19, 21, 23, 80, 206
Four Gates Breathing, 36-37
Four-Six Stance, 24, 110, 118, 169, 172, 199
Functions of the Sword, 2
Geography, 16
Golden Rooster Stands on One Leg Stance,
    25, 109, 131, 149, 195
Gongfu, 1, 23, 33, 101, 192, 194, 196, 198,
    201
Grips, 21
Hamper, 70, 194
Hard, 2-3, 17, 27-28, 33, 53, 99, 194, 196,
    206
Hinder, 66, 71, 196-197, 200
Historical Survey, 7, 9, 11
Hold the Moon Against the Chest, 131, 154
Horse Stance, 23-24, 104, 121, 146, 177,
    196
Hubei Province, 52, 194
Impede, 70, 194
Inspecting the Sword, 4
Intercept, 59, 71, 77, 89, 109, 111-112, 140,
    155, 162-163, 188, 195, 197, 200
Internal, 7, 18-20, 27-31, 37, 53, 59-69,
Internal Power, 7, 20, 53
Internal Styles, 19, 27-28
Jian, 1-3, 14-17, 21, 24, 37, 78, 81, 104,
    139, 150, 176
Key Words, 52-53, 55, 57, 59, 61, 63, 65,
    67, 69, 71, 73, 75, 77, 79
King Wen of Zhou, 101, 196
Left and Right Horizontal Pull, 80
Left and Right Step Over Obstacles, 94
Left and Right Wheel Sword, 150-151
Left Circle and Twist Sword, 81
Left Neutralize and File the Wrist, 184
Left Neutralizing and Stab Forward, 180
Left Sweep, 83-84, 111-112
Left Sweep, Right Sweep, 83-84, 111-112
Left Whirlwind, 88, 125-126, 182-183
Lift, 24, 30, 34, 41, 45-46, 51-52, 63, 82,
    94-95

Little Chief Star, 85-86, 113-114, 124
Liu He Ba Fa, 27
Long Range, 2, 13-14, 20, 153, 192, 198
Long Weapons, 7
Martial Qigong, 26, 28
Matching, 178-188
Matching Practice, 178-188
Meditation, 17, 27, 206
Mentality, 100
Middle Range, 16-17, 20, 52
Mountain Climbing Stance, 24
Muscular Strength, 20-21
Names of Swords, 1
Neutralizing, 18, 52-53, 76, 80, 180
Northern Sword, 19, 52
Obstruct, 71, 196
Ohm's Law, 24
Part the Grass in Search of the Snake, 89-90
Physical Body, 17-18, 26-28
Pluck, 60-61, 197, 200
Point, 2, 5, 14, 23, 45-46, 65, 179, 193, 198
Power, 26-33
Press Down, 73, 128, 201
Pull, 62, 66, 80, 84, 95, 154, 182, 187, 192-193, 196
Push the Boat with the Current, 145-146
Push Ups, 29
Qi Body, 28
Qigong, 18, 26-28, 33, 35, 37, 102
Raise the Screen, 148
Respect, 2, 17
Right Neutralize and Downward Stab, 186
Right Neutralize and Left Pull, 187
Right Sweep, 83-84, 111-112
Right Whirlwind, 87-88, 122, 125, 184-185
Rise, 24, 75, 195, 199
Saber, 1-2, 7, 11, 20-21
Secret Sword, 21, 33, 104-105, 107, 109, 129, 195
Selecting the Sword, 4
Seminars, 189
Send the Bird to the Woods, 131
Shake, 4, 57, 202
Sheath, 5-6, 8, 16, 195
Sheathing the Sword, 5-6
Shi Xiang Zi, 100-101
Shoot the Geese, 155, 160
Short Range, 7
Short Weapons, 2, 7, 17, 20-21
Side Cut, 79, 83, 95, 194
Sink, 38, 77, 192
Sink the Qi, 38
Slide, 5-6, 16, 33, 56, 62-67, 71, 82-83, 85
Sliding Block, 20
Smear, 66-67, 196, 198, 201

Soft, 3, 7, 27-28, 33, 76, 80, 206
Soft-Hard, 28
Southern Sword, 19, 52
Spear, 2, 7, 17, 63, 120
Split, 54, 197
Stab, 8, 55-56, 59, 64, 71,
Step Forward and Close with Sword, 104
Sticking, 13, 18-19, 32-33, 52-53, 80, 93
Sticking and Coiling Training, 32
Swaying, 57, 66, 197
Sweep, 58, 83-84, 111-112, 198
Swing Training, 31
Sword Proverbs, 7
Sword Secret Breathing, 37
Sword Sequences, 1, 99, 197
Sword Structure, 12-13, 15-16
Sword Way, 17
Taiji Sword Qigong, 18, 33, 37
Taijiquan, 17-18, 24, 27, 33, 42, 99, 101,
Tassel, 16, 195
Terminology, 53
The Bird Flying Over the Waterfall, 147
The Black Dragon Waves Its Tail, 132
The Black Dragon Wraps Around the Post, 169-170
The Blue Dragon Waves Its Claws, 156
The Dragonfly Touches the Water, 118
The Fair Lady Weaves with Shuttle, 165
The Fairy Shows the Way, 105, 172
The Lion Shakes Its Head, 91, 135-136
The Night Demon Gauges the Depth of the Sea, 154
The Phoenix Spreads Its Wings, 121, 156
The Rhino Looks at the Moon, 155
The Roc Spreads Its Wings, 152
The Shooting Star Chasing the Moon, 146
The Spirit Cat Catches the Mouse, 116
The Swallow Dips Its Beak in the Water, 110
The Swallow Enters the Nest, 119-120
The Swallow Picks up Mud with Its Beak, 151
The Tiger Holds Its Head, 138
The White Ape Offers Fruit, 161
The White Tiger Waves Its Tail, 166
The Wild Horse Jumps the Stream, 139
The Wind Blows the Lotus Leaf, 133-134
The Yellow Bee Enters the Hole, 115
Three Rings Envelop the Moon, 106
Thrust, 8, 16, 32, 55-56
Tip of the Sword, 4, 6
To Hold a Tablet, 175
Turn Body and Rein in the Horse, 140
Two Brains, 26
Types of Swords, 14
Upward and Downward Yin and Yang, 48

Virtues, 17, 21
Waiting for a Fish, 127
Wash, 74, 201
Wind Blows Away the Plum Flowers, 173-174
Windlass, 30
Wrap, 69, 192, 197, 200
Wudang Mountain, 52, 201
Wuji, 34, 103, 201
Wuji Breathing, 34
Xingyiquan, 28, 206
Yangtze River, 52, 192, 201
Yongquan Breathing, 35-36
Zhang, San-Feng, 99

Books & Videos from YMAA

YMAA Publication Center Books

B004R/671   *Ancient Chinese Weapons—A Martial Artist's Guide*
B005R/574   *Qigong for Health and Martial Arts—Exercises and Meditation (formerly Chi Kung—Health & Martial Arts)*
B006/017   *Northern Shaolin Sword*
B007R/434   *Tai Chi Theory & Martial Power—Advanced Yang Style (formerly Advanced Yang Style Tai Chi Chuan, v.1)*
B008R/442   *Tai Chi Chuan Martial Applications—Advanced Yang Style (formerly Advanced Yang Style Tai Chi Chuan, v.2)*
B009/041   *Analysis of Shaolin Chin Na—Instructor's Manual for all Martial Styles*
B010R/523   *Eight Simple Qigong Exercises for Health—The Eight Pieces of Brocade*
B011R/507   *The Root of Chinese Qigong—Secrets for Health, Longevity, & Enlightenment*
B012/068   *Muscle/Tendon Changing and Marrow/Brain Washing Chi Kung—The Secret of Youth*
B013/084   *Hsing Yi Chuan—Theory and Applications*
B014R/639   *The Essence of Taiji Qigong—The Internal Foundation of Taijiquan (formerly Tai Chi Chi Kung)*
B015R/426   *Arthritis—The Chinese Way of Healing and Prevention (formerly Qigong for Arthritis)*
B016/254   *Chinese Qigong Massage—General Massage*
B017R/345   *How to Defend Yourself—Effective & Practical Martial Arts Strategies*
B018/289   *The Tao of Bioenergetics—East-West*
B019R/337   *Tai Chi Chuan—24 & 48 Postures with Martial Applications (formerly Simplified Tai Chi Chuan)*
B020/300   *Baguazhang—Emei Baguazhang*
B021/36x   *Comprehensive Applications of Shaolin Chin Na—The Practical Defense of Chinese Seizing Arts for All Styles*
B022/378   *Taiji Chin Na—The Seizing Art of Taijiquan*
B023/319   *Professional Budo—Ethics, Chivalry, and the Samurai Code*
B024/272   *Song of a Water Dragon—Biography of He Yi An*
B025/353   *The Essence of Shaolin White Crane—Martial Power and Qigong*
B026/450   *Openings—A Zen Joke Guide for Serious Problem Solving*
B027/361   *Wisdom's Way—101 Tales of Chinese Wit*
B028/493   *Chinese Fast Wrestling for Fighting—The Art of San Shou Kuai Jiao*
B029/37x   *Chinese Fitness—A Mind/Body Approach*
B030/515   *Back Pain—Chinese Qigong for Healing and Prevention*
B031/582   *108 Insights into Tai Chi Chuan—A String of Pearls*
B032/647   *The Tai Chi Book—Refining and Enjoying a Lifetime of Practice*
B033/655   *The Martial Arts Athlete—Mental and Physical Conditioning for Peak Performance*
B034/68x   *Taijiquan, Classical Yang Style—The Complete Form and Qigong*
B035/71x   *Tai Chi Secrets of the Ancient Masters—Selected Readings with Commentary*
B036/744   *Taiji Sword, Classical Yang Style—The Complete Form, Qigong, and Applications*
B037/760   *Power Body—Injury Prevention, Rehabilitation, and Sports Performance Enhancement*

YMAA Publication Center Videotapes

T001/181   *Yang Style Tai Chi Chuan—and Its Applications*
T002/19x   *Shaolin Long Fist Kung Fu—Lien Bu Chuan and Its Applications*
T003/203   *Shaolin Long Fist Kung Fu—Gung Li Chuan and Its Applications*
T004/211   *Analysis of Shaolin Chin Na*
T005/22x   *Eight Simple Qigong Exercises for Health—The Eight Pieces of Brocade*
T006/238   *The Essence of Taiji Qigong—The Internal Foundation of Taijiquan*
T007/246   *Arthritis—The Chinese Way of Healing and Prevention*
T008/327   *Chinese Qigong Massage—Self Massage*
T009/335   *Chinese Qigong Massage—With a Partner*
T010/343   *How to Defend Yourself 1—Unarmed Attack*
T011/351   *How to Defend Yourself 2—Knife Attack*
T012/386   *Comprehensive Applications of Shaolin Chin Na 1*
T013/394   *Comprehensive Applications of Shaolin Chin Na 2*
T014/256   *Shaolin Long Fist Kung Fu—Yi Lu Mai Fu & Er Lu Mai Fu and Their Applications*
T015/264   *Shaolin Long Fist Kung Fu—Shi Zi Tang and Its Applications*
T016/408   *Taiji Chin Na*
T017/280   *Emei Baguazhang 1—Basic Training, Qigong, Eight Palms, & Their Applications*
T018/299   *Emei Baguazhang 2—Swimming Body & Its Applications*
T019/302   *Emei Baguazhang 3—Bagua Deer Hook Sword & Its Applications*
T020/310   *Xingyiquan—The Twelve Animal Patterns & Their Applications*
T021/329   *Simplified Tai Chi Chuan—Simplified 24 Postures & Standard 48 Postures*
T022/469   *Sun Style Taijiquan—With Applications*
T023/477   *Wu Style Taijiquan—With Applications*
T024/485   *Tai Chi Chuan & Applications—Simplified 24 Postures with Applications & Standard 48 Postures*
T025/604   *Shaolin Long Fist Kung Fu—Xiao Hu Yuan (Roaring Tiger Fist) and Its Applications*
T026/612   *White Crane Hard Qigong—The Essence of Shaolin White Crane*
T027/620   *White Crane Soft Qigong—The Essence of Shaolin White Crane*
T028/566   *Back Pain—Chinese Qigong for Healing & Prevention*
T029/590   *The Scientific Foundation of Chinese Qigong—A Lecture by Dr. Yang, Jwing-Ming*
T030/752   *Taijiquan, Classical Yang Style—The Complete Form and Qigong*
T031/817   *Taiji Sword, Classical Yang Style—The Complete Form, Qigong, and Applications*

YMAA Publication Center   楊氏東方文化出版中心

4354 Washington Street • Boston, MA 02131
1-800-669-8892 • ymaa@aol.com • www.ymaa.com